SIGNET BOOKS

THE SECOND-HAND SHOP
GUIDE TO LONDON

THE SECOND-HAND SHOPPING GUIDE TO LONDON

Graham Parker

A SIGNET BOOK

SIGNET

Published by the Penguin Group
Penguin Books Ltd, 27 Wrights Lane, London W8 5TZ, England
Penguin Books USA Inc., 375 Hudson Street, New York, New York 10014, USA
Penguin Books Australia Ltd, Ringwood, Victoria, Australia
Penguin Books Canada Ltd, 10 Alcorn Avenue, Toronto, Ontario, Canada M4V 3B2
Penguin Books (NZ) Ltd, 182–190 Wairau Road, Auckland 10, New Zealand

Penguin Books Ltd, Registered Offices: Harmondsworth, Middlesex, England

First published by Michael Joseph 1995
Published in Signet 1996
1 3 5 7 9 10 8 6 4 2

Printed in England by Clays Ltd, St Ives plc

CONTENTS

ACKNOWLEDGEMENTS

Thanks to the unfailing Stephen Bordoley, as well as Hugh Balchin, the Hon. Christopher Bellew, Adele Mason and Freddie Stockdale, Danielle Winter and Alan Yoshioka for their help and companionship during research.

INTRODUCTION

The taboo of shopping for second-hand goods has long gone. The post-Victorian idea of stingy ferreting through musty rags or settling for soiled cast-offs no longer springs to mind, as the concept of pre-used has been elevated from shabby to chic.

The idea of writing a book about second-hand shopping came to me when I found a cashmere Burberry scarf on the pavement outside Golders Green crematorium in the middle of winter. I decided then and there that some second-hand items were higher in quality than anything I could afford to buy new. Thereafter I discovered old furniture, picking up things like an Edwardian bureau, Victorian table or Sixties bookcase and sanding, painting or polishing until something respectable emerged. Tweed jackets and designer shirts were a short leap away, and then books, records and videos.

Buying second-hand embodies a lot of what the environmentally conscious 1990s are all about. The age of **recycling** dictates that we re-use kitchen scraps, bottles, cans, newspapers and cardboard – and the principle can easily be extended to other aspects of our lives. Furniture and clothes were, in the main, better made thirty or forty years ago – Victorian wardrobes are sturdy and attractive; tweed jackets seem to improve with age, and now that records are no longer pressed, buying pre-used ones is your only option. With a dab of glue, a coat of varnish or a needle and thread, you can breathe new life into other people's cast-offs, and create something attractive, long-lasting and useful.

But recycling doesn't mean skimping where **style** is concerned. The second-hand revolution has already left its mark on the 1990s, a retro-spective decade where fashion often takes the lead from what's already happened – whether in the Sixties, Fifties or earlier. Clothes, music and furniture from past eras have never been so fashionable and, since they were not mass-produced, buying them means that you can assert your individuality when buying second-hand.

Shopping second-hand is also **cheap**. Compare the cost of new furniture or clothes with their second-hand equivalents; you may need to apply some elbow grease to a sideboard or sewing prowess to a shirt, but the result can make you wonder why major retail chains are still in business. Buying a three-year-old rug is like buying a new one and inflicting three years' wear and tear on it; buying second-hand books equates to purchasing them new, reading them and putting them on your bookshelf. It just costs an awful lot less.

Of course, second-hand shopping is more unpredictable than buying new, as you cannot go with a clear vision of what you want to buy in mind – the make, style, colour or size, the particular novel you are after, or the specific size, shape and finish of the mahogany sewing box you covet – but the uncovering of unexpected treasures has a charm all its own.

This book was devised for people who want a bargain, but also for people who enjoy collecting, restoring and enjoying pre-used things. It's essentially a budget guide, but is based on value for money rather than just bargain buys – there are some more expensive shops selling quality antiques listed here, but they always represent a decent deal compared with the overinflated prices of some Islington or Kensington dealers.

The written word

There are dozens of **newspapers and magazines** that deal solely in second-hand matter. If you're patient and have the time, they can be the source of some terrific bargains – but you do need to be patient, as you often have to do a lot of phoning around only to find that the sofa for £25 has already been snapped up. Likewise, you may make an appointment to view, only to find that the dining table you're after is too big to fit through your front door.

Loot is a daily free-ads newspaper with a noticeboard service, offering 'everything for everyone, everyday' and featuring classified ads selling everything from antique pieces and musical instruments through to cheap records, clothes and cheap furniture. The *London Weekly Advertiser*, *Exchange and Mart* and the *Bargain Hunter* are publications in the same vein.

Commercial local papers are a source of no-strings buys in furniture, clothes or records – try papers attached to swankier areas like the *Ham and High*, the *Islington Gazette* or the *Kensington and Chelsea Gazette*, where some forgotten heirlooms may be up for grabs.

Free local papers may likewise come up with bargains, with the plus that you don't have to travel far to view. If you don't have freebie papers pushed through your front door regularly, ring your local council for details of available publications.

If you have a particular interest, there are always **specialist newspapers and magazines** that carry small ads selling off equipment – for instance, the *Stage and Screen Today* has ads for cast-off magic props, feather boas, costumes and wigs, as well as publishing announcements of theatrical auctions. For pre-used musical instruments, try the *New Musical Express* or *Melody Maker*, or the more specialist *Guitar*, *Guitar World* and yearly *Guitar Buyers Guide*; if you want to buy second-hand computers, there's a bewildering array of titles, like *MacWorld*, *Computer Buyer*, *Computer Shopper*, *Micro Computer Mart* and *PC Mart*, where you can find a range of second-hand hard- and software. Philately enthusiasts should consult *Gibbons Stamp Monthly* and *Stamp Magazine*, and the *Book Collector* lists books and magazines for sale. All these specialist papers and magazines are available at good newsagents.

Scraping the bottom of the barrel

If you're really keen for a rock-bottom bargain, there are lots of other ways to pick up second-hand goods beyond shops and trawling through newspapers. There are regular **jumble sales** in local church or scout halls and **car boot sales** in neighbourhood car parks where prices are very low. Keep your eyes open for **notices** in the windows of local shops and the large noticeboards behind the check-outs of supermarkets where people will place ads if they want to sell off unwanted furniture. Often **video shops** will get rid of rental videos cheaply, **libraries** will sell off books for next to nothing and **music libraries** will sell libretti, tapes and CDs for a song.

The cheapest way of recycling other people's unwanted possessions is by monitoring the many **skips** that appear on London's residential streets. During flat conversions, you'll probably find rotted floorboards and building waste, but pieces of furniture, carpet and underfelt will often show up, just waiting for some DIY attention. My flatmate's mother plucked out of a skip a Thirties mirror in very good condition, which needed nothing more than a quick wipe over and a nail to hang it on the wall. You should of course check with the skip's owner to ensure that the items in it have been truly abandoned, otherwise you may be helping yourself – illegally – to someone else's possessions.

Price tags

Note that the prices of goods used within the listings of this guide are indications only of a shop's pricing policy and can't be taken as gospel. Obviously, one of the joys of shopping in second-hand shops is the unpredictability of the stock – a shop may feature an Armani shirt for £5 one week and have nothing but cheap department store cast-offs the next, so the prices and items quoted here are a very rough guide.

It is up to you as to the buyer to be happy with how much you pay for an item – there are no set guidelines that say you should only pay under £10 for a 1960s glazed coffee pot, so it comes down to your perception of value and how much you think something is worth. You get better at judging goods the more you shop, and after a while you find yourself appraising the grain of wood, the cut of crystal or the feel of material. Haggling comes with experience and looses its ability to be a life-threatening misdemeanour.

Let the buyer beware

When you buy something in a shop, a contract of sale will arise with the seller, whether an individual, a charity or company, even without a receipt or other written proof. Proving that there was a contract and deciding what its terms were in the absence of written proof could be difficult and you should always, at least, ask for a receipt.

Do not be fobbed off with assurances that any item (especially an electrical appliance) is still covered by some part of a manufacturer's guarantee, and beware of unusually long guarantee periods promised to you by any seller. Your rights against a seller are only as good as his ability to carry out his promises.

When you buy goods, ask for a specific description to be put on the bill or receipt that you are given. By and large, if an item is described as, say, a hot water bottle, then that is what it must be. If it is not, then there will be breach of the Sale of Goods Act requirements.

The item should be of 'satisfactory quality', although you cannot expect second-hand items to be in new condition. For instance, if buying a second-hand radio you would not expect its case to be in pristine condition but you would expect it to operate so that it picks up the wave bands shown. This is subject to the important exception that the seller can (prior to your agreeing to buy the item – not afterwards) reduce his obligations with the regard to satisfactory quality by either pointing out defects or for the defects to be self-evident (such as a scratch on the case of the radio or a missing aerial). Do be careful to examine any stickers on the goods that might be intended to draw defects to your attention. Unless you are specifically told (either by the seller verbally or by a sticker on the item), an item, however cheap, which does not carry out its main function is unlikely to be of satisfactory quality (e.g. a kettle that refuses to boil at all).

The item should also be fit for its purpose: this will apply if you ask the seller whether the item can perform some task. If it is important to you, try and get the required attribute referred to on the receipt (e.g. FM/AM radio).

If an item turns out to be defective on further detailed examination, you should as soon as possible attempt to 'reject' the item by taking it back or getting in touch with the seller to point out that it is defective. Despite what the sellers frequently say, there is no right to insist on having something repaired, although the seller may well offer or agree to a repair being made. Return speedily to avoid being assumed to have accepted the item and therefore losing the right to reject it. By and large, your best approach is to try and negotiate amicably with the shopkeeper for the return of the item or a rebate on the price where there has been a genuine misunderstanding or failure. You may well agree to have it repaired and parts of it replaced, and as a result of a recent change in the law (1994) you will not lose your right to return the item and demand a refund of what you have paid merely by asking for or agreeing to such repair. This needs to be a matter of your judgement depending on the circumstances. If you choose to have the item repaired somewhere else (having lost faith in the original seller), then the cost of having it repaired is – at least theoretically – recoverable from the original seller.

This is the briefest outline, for guidance only, of some parts of the law relating to the sale of goods. It must not be relied upon as providing legal advice in respect of any purchase you make, and you may need to seek specialized legal help from a Citizens Advice Bureau, Law Centre or solicitor.

Every effort has been made to ensure that the informaton in this book is as accurate as possible at the time of going to press. If you have any corrections or suggestions, please write to me c/o Michael Joseph Ltd., 27 Wrights Lane, London W8 5TZ.

SPECIALIZED SHOPS

ARCHITECTURAL SALVAGE

Thatcherism turned the nation into a hysterical frenzy of chiselling yuppies who wanted nothing more than an open fireplace, Persian rug and ceiling rose in every room, spawning a range of fireplace, stripped pine door and specialist ecclesiastical salvage shops a million miles from the grimy old architectural salvage warehouses of yesteryear. For those who like a more hands-on approach, there is still a range of old-fashioned salvage places, taking in builder's yards where you fossick amongst cisterns and radiators.

Amazing Grates
61 High Road, East Finchley N2
(0181) 883 9590
This cheekily named shop stores a wealth of Victorian and Edwardian fireplaces and cast-iron grates, ranging from simple stripped or painted pine models to fantastic Victorian rococo. Prices are reasonably high, but you'll find beautifully restored pieces: they had a small iron grate and firepiece for £345, a cast-iron insert and wood mantel in painted timber at £399, a complete cast-iron insert and surround for £460, and a corbel and cast-iron tiled insert and marble fireplace for £750. Grates range from £200 for a simple model. Brass Victorian tongs are also in stock, as well as new reproduction fireplaces.

Churchill's Architectural Salvage
206 and 212 Old Kent Road, Southwark SE1 (0171) 708 4308
This shop is a specialist in antique fireplaces, decorative items, period bath fittings, cast-iron bed frames, decorative ironwork, bathroom fittings and pine furniture, and sells a range of marble fire surrounds and inserts, garden furniture, a few mirrors, brass fittings, tiles and some furniture. You'll find oddments like taps for £15, chamber pots at £15 and cast-iron double beds for £450. They supply missing bars, bricks etc. A wooden unrestored fireplace surround for £50, a cast-iron restored fireplace for £80, marble and slate ones for £200, and cast-iron inserts for £60.

Crocodile Antiques
336 Muswell Hill Broadway, Muswell Hill N10 (0181) 365 3424
In a courtyard next to an art gallery and shop, this architectural salvage centre has a supply of Victorian and Georgian fireplaces, along with cast-iron radiators, benches, chairs, tables, bird baths, statues, and terracotta pots from Thailand and Mexico. You'll find things like cast-iron inserts from £80, an ornate 2ft-high gilt carved mirror for a dressing table for £125, a Thirties wood mantel and surround with inlaid mirror for £225 or a Victorian marble clock for £45.

The Fire Works
100 Old Kent Road, Southwark SE1
(0171) 635 6659
This small shop near Queens Road Peckham British Rail station carries

mainly Victorian fireplace inserts and surrounds, as well as a few Georgian pieces. Inserts start from £275 for a typical 30-inch model, and marble surrounds go for £300 upwards. There is a reasonable range, all renovated and assembled by the owner.

Fireplace Company
61 Essex Road, Islington N1
(0171) 359 8179
Very unusual grandiose pieces are sold in this shop, which itself has a rather theatrical and somewhat decadent decor. They had a semicircular wood frame window, a huge white marble fireplace with tiled insert, pillars for £250, an elaborately carved decorative chair, plus some churchy items like stained glass, Gothic stone arches, urns and marble obelisks.

Fireplaces
178 Bowes Road, Palmers Green N13
(0181) 889 1440
Right on the North Circular, this basic fireplace shop stocks reconditioned cast-iron inserts starting at £75 for a small one, up to £900 for a register (mantelpiece, insert and surround). The wooden surrounds are generally new, but a well-restored Victorian pine surround costs around £250.

Mantels
9 Lavender Hill, Battersea SW11
(0171) 585 2256
A shop on two floors stuffed with an array of inserts, marble and pine surrounds, all well restored and ready to install. Inserts start from £400, and the pine surrounds go for £300 up. A huge elaborately carved French white marble surround was £675.

Jonathan Murray Fireplaces
358 Upper Richmond Road, Mortlake SW14 (0181) 876 7934
A fireplace specialist which has mainly new inserts and surrounds (in an old style), but also stocks some unusual antique pieces. A range of stripped and restored Victorian pine surrounds with some intricate carvings start at around £150.

The Old Door and Fireplace Company
67–69 Essex Road, Islington N1
(0171) 226 0910
This shop deals in elaborate cast-iron inserts, marble friezes, brass door handles, letter-boxes, candles, marble and stone surrounds, and brass grates, all in good condition.

The Old Fire Station
306–312 Old Kent Road, Southwark SE1
(0171) 703 7437
This stunning building – the area's original Victorian fire station, complete with tiles, doors and the odd model fireman – stocks stoves, fireplaces, garden furniture and general architectural salvage. Marble surrounds range from £200 to thousands, wooden ones £60–600, while a cast-iron insert will set you back £95–600. Gilt mirrors sell for around £160, small enamelled solid fuel stoves from £150, Victorian radiators from £50. Chimney pots start at £10. The owner is proud of his building restoration work and will give you a guided tour if you ask.

Phoenix Fireplaces
94 Old Kent Road, New Cross SE14
(0171) 252 8047
The range of fireplaces here is not enormous, but there is a high turnover and the prices are very reasonable. Typical Victorian inserts start at £200, pine surrounds at £250 and marble surrounds at £350, with a fitting service from around £125.

Timberland
189 High Street, Willesden NW10
(0181) 459 2947
Next to the New Testament Church of God, this Dickensian junkyard on the corner of Hawthorn Road sells a self-service selection of fireplaces, wrought-iron work, sinks, flooring, doors, roof tiles, chimney pots, bathroom suites, radiators, wrought-iron spiral staircases, toilet cisterns and the like.

Tsar Architectural
487 Liverpool Road, Holloway N7
(0171) 609 4238
Tsar is a marvellous shop, stuffed with all manner of brass bits and pieces, lamps, tiles, stained glass, mirrors, hooks, knobs, fireplaces and inserts. All the brass is restored to gleaming newness, and there are doorknobs starting at £8 and hooks for £3. Hanging china light fittings start at £15, and wall-mounted ones from only £10. Cast-iron inserts go for around £125, and there was a cast-iron surround and insert for £175. There's also some furniture – usually on the pavement outside – including bookcases, sideboards, cabinets and umbrella stands in various stages of disrepair.

Universal Providers
86 Golborne Road, Notting Hill W10
This is architectural salvage on a grand scale, with bits and pieces that look as if they've been uplifted from Brideshead. You'll find wrought-iron fancy balustrades, marble fireplaces, pillars and sundry pieces of grand carving, huge mantelpiece mirrors, Victorian tiles, marble-top tables and panelling. It's not cheap, but the experience is uplifting.

Victorian Pine
298 Brockley Road, Brockley SE4
(0181) 691 7162
This period pine door specialist stocks mainly reclaimed doors – plain, panelled or with stained-glass inserts – as well as a small selection of sundries like banisters, fireplaces (from £70), old church pews (from £120) and Victorian chests of drawers (from £150). The doors are hefty and generally need renovating, but start at a very reasonable £40. Free local delivery depending on how much spent. Open daily.

BOOKS

See also Charity Shops, Junk Shops, Auction Rooms *and* Markets

London's second-hand bookshops are renowned for their variety, quality and sheer profusion – Charing Cross Road is the undisputed world-famous leader in the field; but you can still pick up some cheap second-hand reading matter in the less well-known parts of the centre or some of the surprisingly good suburban shops which have regularly updated stock and throwaway paperbacks for as little as 50p. There's also the other end of the market – fine antiquarian tomes and first editions, both of which are catered for around Covent Garden.

Any Amount of Books
62 Charing Cross Road, Covent Garden WC2 (0171) 240 8140
A shop dealing in modern first editions and antiquarian books, with an interesting selection of both fiction and non-fiction. It's smaller than the other bookshops along this road, and although limited to a certain degree is still worth the browsing time. The paperback fiction sells at about half the new retail price of the book, and features nearly new copies of contemporary authors. Outside is always a rack of paperbacks for £1 – standard practice along Charing Cross Road to draw the punters in.

Archive Secondhand Books and Music
83 Bell Street, Marylebone NW1 (0171) 402 8212
This bookshop is straight out of Charles Dickens' day, with mountains of dusty cardboard boxes spilling over with paperback and hardback books and sheet music. Religious and political books are squeezed into bookcases down the stairway, and the basement is awash with sheet music, scores, libretti and music compendiums. Upstairs is general fiction and non-fiction, with an acceptably musty smell. Outside are bargain bins, with paperback books from 50p and hardbacks from £1.50.

Ballantyne and Date
37 Coptic Street, Bloomsbury WC1 (0171) 242 4249
A specialist art bookseller, concentrating on design in its many forms – illustration, the decorative arts, photography, furniture, painting. Novels outside start at £1 for paperbacks and £2 for hardbacks.

Bell, Book and Radmall
4 Cecil Court, Covent Garden WC2 (0171) 240 2161
This excellent collectors' shop stocks mostly nineteenth and twentieth-century literature and poetry, arranged alphabetically by author. There is a very comprehensive crime section, as well as sci-fi and fantasy downstairs. Some leather-bound rare books.

Benedict's Books
92 Lillie Road, Fulham SW6 (0171) 385 4426
Just by the North End Road junction

in a down-at-heel block of shops, this raises its head above them all, with a quirky jumble of sundry books alongside old vases, glasses, bits of china, baskets dotted around between the books, piled high on shelves, bookcases and cabinets. You have to step over piles of books to get to whatever you want to see, but you're rewarded by a selection of fiction, art, military and geography. Outside are piles of dirty battered paperbacks for 50p, alongside a rack with better-kept books for £1.

Bookmongers
404 Coldharbour Lane, Brixton SE5
(0181) 738 4225
This interesting little bookshop is filled floor to ceiling with a good collection of general books, and a large selection of novels, both classic and modern. Books outside go for only 20p, and paperbacks inside start from £1 and hardbacks from £2.

Books Bought Bookshop
357 King's Road, Chelsea SW3
(0171) 352 9376
This small shop on a bend in the King's Road is highly unobtrusive – but once inside you'll find you can pick up a host of fiction books in near perfect condition at a third of their original published price. Fiction paperbacks start at around £1 for John Irving, Margaret Atwood, Forster, Dickens *et al.* and hardback biographies, poetry, aviation and politics books start at around £3. A 27-volume set of leather-bound Victorian parliamentary debates cost £100. The owner offers a 10 percent discount on Saturdays and a 20 percent discount on Sundays.

Books For Cooks
4 Blenheim Crescent, Notting Hill W11
(0171) 221 1992
This exceptional bookshop focuses on one thing – food. The 4000 titles in stock at any one time extol the virtues of it, tell you how to prepare it and show you what to drink with it, and the shop even has regular demonstrations in its kitchen at the back and a regular three-course lunch at £10. The many facets of victuals covered by the books range from wholefood and vegan to historical recipes, microwave grub, bread-baking and the like. The owner can give advice on where to eat in London – which chefs are away on holiday etc. – and promises to obtain cookbooks from anywhere in the world if requested. The first floor has a kitchen and seating area available for private functions.

Books 'N' Bits
28 Brockley Road, Brockley SE4
(0181) 692 9480
This bookshop just by Brockley Cross is a haven for a cheap read. Paperbacks – everything from Wilbur Smith to Mills & Boon by way of Dickens and Thackeray – start at only 40p, and hardbacks from £1. There are also records from 50p – Andy Stewart and Max Bygraves releases typically feature strongly, and a quick flick through might turn up a David Cassidy or Diana Ross LP from way back. China and glassware comes mostly in the form of lurid Seventies shapeless ashtrays and vases – but a Royal Doulton trinket box was only £5.

Bookscene
208 King Street, Hammersmith W6
This tiny bookshop is a five- to ten-minute walk from Hammersmith tube station, but is worth the effort for the interesting selection of paperbacks it stocks, mostly from £1. The major categories are romance, thriller, war, non-fiction, general fiction and biography, with a bargain

bin outside with certain titles for 30p. Porn magazines from £1, comics from 75p.

The Charing Cross Bookshop
56 Charing Cross Road, Covent Garden WC2 (0171) 836 3697
Outside this well-established shop, there are paperback blockbusters and romances for £1 on a bookcase in the doorway. Inside is a good, varied selection of theatre, art, paperback literature, poetry, biography and history, with the leather-bound antiquarian books tucked away behind a counter, guarded by an assistant. The basement smells rather damp, but has an excellent, and somewhat older range of literature, history and travel, with a good range of non-fiction from quite new to very old books. Under the stairs is a tiny room selling off books for 50p or five for £2. There are regular basement sales.

Circa
144 Stoke Newington Church Street, Stoke Newington N16 (0171) 249 9775
A New Age place with a selection of glassware, prints and cards, and a welcome book selection at the back of the shop, not large but interesting. There is mainly modern fiction, with a few classics thrown in, with paperbacks starting at £2.

CECIL COURT

An interesting excursion into London's specialist book trade is Covent Garden's narrow Cecil Court leading from Charing Cross Road to St Martin's Lane.

Watkins Books, at nos. 19–21, is a good starting point, with a fascinating collection dealing with the occult and mystic specialist. Entering children's specialist *Marchpane* at no. 16 is like stepping back to Lewis Carroll's time.

At no. 18 are *Reg and Philip Remington*, who carry only travel books, as does the *Traveller's Bookshop*, which had the entire Baedeker editions at no. 25, and *Alan Brett* at no. 24, with a sundry collection of atlases, maps, prints and rare books.

The performing arts are represented by *Pleasure of Past Times* at no. 11, the specialist performing arts place, *Dance Books*, at no. 9, and *Travis and Emery*, at no. 17, with its music biographies, libretti and sheet music.

Coffeehouse Bookshop
139 Greenwich South Street, Greenwich SE10 (0181) 692 3885
This small local bookshop stocks a bit of everything and makes an interesting browse if you're in the area. Stacked up paperbacks go from £1.50 with everything from poetry, modern fiction to sci fi, and dozens of Mills & Boons. Comics like *Zit*, *Photoplay*, *Sky* and *Commando* from £1.25, and records from £1.50.

Curios
127 Stoke Newington Church Street, Stoke Newington N16 (0171) 275 8638
A tiny second-hand bookshop – more a bookshelf and a trestle table, really – featuring mainly modern fiction and blockbusters in paperback, plus numerous big names like Muriel Spark, E.M. Forster, Colin Forbes, Stephen King, Joseph Conran and Anthony Burgess. Paperbacks average around £2 each.

Dance Books
9 Cecil Court, Covent Garden WC2
(0171) 836 2314
The stock in this specialist shop focuses on dance – ballet, human movement, folk, ballroom, ancient Greek and hip hop – also taking in diet, nutrition, technique and the like. There are photos of famous dancers, theatre programmes, lithographs and posters, as well as a range of records of stage shows and films from £4.

Francis Edwards
13 Great Newport Street (off Charing Cross Road), Covent Garden WC2
(0171) 379 7692
A naval and milititary book specialist close to Leicester Square tube station, tucked around the corner from Charing Cross Road and next to Quinto, Francis Edwards keeps a stock of anything related to military campaigns and characters, especially British ones – Indian campaigns, Boer War, Pretoria – and many first editions, starting from £10 up to £100s.

Keith Fawkes
1–3 Flask Walk, Hampstead NW3
(0171) 435 0614
This atmospherically creaky old bookshop just off Hampstead's classy high road on a flagstone pedestrianized street has floor-to-ceiling bookshelves crammed with books that seem to have been here for ever. There are good, well-ordered selections – especially in the hardback field – of fiction, art, literature and transport, making this a terrific shop to spend a couple of hours browsing. There's also a selection of rare books on art, history and literature.

Fitzjohn's Books
27a Northways Parade, College Crescent, Swiss Cottage NW3
(0171) 722 9864
Near Swiss Cottage tube station, this narrow shop at the bottom of Fitzjohn's Avenue has a small but interesting general selection of books, including quite a few German language novels.

For Books
Elephant and Castle shopping centre, Elephant and Castle SE1 (0171) 703 2876
On the ground floor of the hideous Seventies shopping centre, this excellent bookshop makes an unexpected find, and although not dirt cheap, has a fascinating and wide collection, with especially good politics and war sections. History, biography, psychology, lit crit and art are all here, next to the good range of general fiction. Although you can pay up to £5 for a paperback, it will be in mint condition.

W.A. Foster and Son
134 Chiswick High Road, Chiswick W4
(0171) 995 2768
An olde-worlde bow-fronted Georgian building fronts a shop crammed with an assortment of antique and second-hand books, from art books to paperbacks about teacup fortune telling. A nice shop to have a quiet weekend browse.

Gloucester Road Bookshop
123 Gloucester Road, South Kensington SW7 (0171) 370 3503
A brilliant bookshop down from Gloucester Road tube station with a very good hard- and paperback range of fiction, travel, biography, royalty, lit crit, politics and the arts over two floors. There's a selection of cheap paperbacks in the basement for only 50p and hardbacks that have also been knocked down in price. Open until 10.30p.m. Monday to Friday.

Greenwich Book Time
1 Greenwich South Street, Greenwich SE10
A good selection of general paper-

back fiction in good condition and averaging around £3. They also sell records here from £1 and a few tapes at about the same price.

Charles Higham
Holy Trinity Church, Marylebone Road, Euston NW1 (0171) 387 5282
On the corner of Osnaburgh Street opposite Great Portland Street tube station, this Baroque church specializes in theological tomes. They apparently stock up to 35,000 books at any one time in the aisles of the church and must surely rate as London's most serene shop. Apart from the obvious religious tracts, prayer books, bibles, Church of Ireland doctrines and hymn books, there is a selection of novels and biographies, and books covering travel, architecture of Gothic churches and the English countryside.

Kirkdale Bookshop
272 Sydenham Road, Sydenham SE26 (0181) 778 4701
The ground floor of this surprisingly good suburban bookshop is devoted mainly to new releases, although at the back is a range of first editions, anthologies, general fiction and boxed sets. Downstairs in a typically damp, musty basement is a well-sorted and very good range of fiction and non-fiction. Paperbacks average around £2 each, and hardbacks £4, and there's a half-price table, as well as a 15p clearance table outside.

Marchpane
16 Cecil Court, Covent Garden WC2 (0171) 836 8661
Cecil Court's children's specialist is Marchpane, a joy to browse in and recollect what you used to read when you were a little nipper. There's everything here from A.A. Milne, yearly annuals – *Blue Peter*, the Muppets, *Boy's Own* – Grimm's and Andersen's fairy tales, *Alice in Wonderland* engravings from £10 and educational books.

Oxfam Bookshop
91 Marylebone High Street, Marylebone W1
This is the only one in the Oxfam chain that specializes in books and sells a small selection of items, but has them neatly – if overzealously – ordered into crime, horror, fantasy, general, sport, health, etc. Fiction paperbacks from 50p, hardbacks from £1.50.

Pleasure of Past Times
11 Cecil Court, Covent Garden WC2 (0171) 836 1142
A wonderful old shop with a year-round carnival atmosphere set up by the actor David Drummond and retaining a very theatrical feel. Everything in this shop has to do with entertainment in bygone years: music halls, circus, old annuals, children's books, Victorian bits and pieces, greeting cards and old Valentines, theatre, dance, playbills, film autographs, old *Empire* front pages, and books about stars and directors.

Popular Book Centre
284 Lewisham High Street, Lewisham SE13 (0181) 690 5110
This bookshop has piles of novels, biographies and magazines, although the subject-matter makes it more of a male preserve. Comics like *Fantazia, Twilight Zone, Fangoria*, and *The Avengers* start at £2.50, mags like *Flex, Karate, Penthouse* and *Start* at £1.50. Paperbacks start at the bargain price of 20p – Mills & Boon, lots of blockbusters, horror, thrillers, war, crime and sci fi. The shop also operates an exchange scheme.

Henry Pordes Books Ltd
58–60 Charing Cross Road, Covent Garden WC2 (0171) 836 9031
This large Charing Cross Road shop features books to do with the arts, whether it be sculpture, Gothic art, Japanese gardens, Toulouse-Lautrec, ships in bottles, golf, antique radios, Dada movement, totalitarian art, birds of the West Indies, Wagner, handwriting or nouveau cinema in Italy. It has modern first editions like a Joe Orton going for £20 or a Hemingway for a bargain £8. On the ground floor are new art and travel books to the right as you walk in alongside a good hardback fiction section. At the back on the ground floor is a small section on travel and lit crit, and there are paperbacks and miscellaneous books downstairs in the basement.

Primrose Hill Books
134 Regent's Park Road, Primrose Hill NW1 (0171) 586 2022
In swanky Primrose Hill village, this excellent shop features second-hand fiction under its awnings for about £1. Inside is new travel, fiction, etc., and, down a perilous wrought-iron staircase, the second-hand basement. There's a very good selection of novels averaging at £3, along with hardback literature, history, travel and the like.

Quinto
48 Charing Cross Road, Covent Garden WC2 (0171) 379 7669
The smell of old books is impregnated on this shop, which has bare floorboards and wooden bookcases floor to ceiling. Upstairs are hardback books of poetry, lit crit, general fiction, as well as cinema, art, music and antiques. A concreted passage containing children's books and militaria leads to the basement where you'll find paperback fiction, and books on economics, sociology, women's studies, education, politics, transport, travel, theology and the like. The irritating thing is that the paperback fiction isn't in alphabetical order, but browsing among the mixed genres can be quite absorbing if you have time up your sleeve. Hardbacks start at around £4.50, paperbacks at £1.

Reg and Philip Remington
18 Cecil Court, Covent Garden WC2 (0171) 836 9771
Discovery and adventure characterize this shop, where the owners have amassed a collection to do with getting out and about in the world – voyages, travel or natural history. You'll typically find works to do with Antarctic penguins, the life of James Cook, T.E. Lawrence, Scott's expeditions, Paul Revere, Marco Polo, wild tribes of the Afghan frontier, or Man-eaters of Kumaon. The books are antiquarian and second-hand and almost all are hardbacks. Also stocks maps and prints.

Ripping Yarns
355 Archway Road, Highgate N6 (0171) 354 0843
Stuffed full of second-hand editions of all sorts, this old-fashioned bookshop also specializes in children's books of yesteryear for toddlers up to mid-teenagers. Enid Blyton, A.A. Milne and Biggles will bring back the odd memory. There are a lot of hardbound classics, along with a wall of softback fiction and specific sections like movies and TV, history, travel, etc. Open seven days a week.

Bernard J. Shapero Rare Books
80 Holland Park, Holland Park W11 (0171) 436 9132
A huge showroom of antiquarian travel books and prints, and a comprehensive selection of thousands of books to do with travel, including

expensive first editions, newish travel guides, natural history books, and books on photography from the air and the like. This is the best selection of travel books in London.

Ian Shipley (Books) Ltd
70 Charing Cross Road, Covent Garden WC2 (0171) 836 4872
This specialist art bookshop features a wide range of editions focusing on the visual arts new and second-hand – fine arts, design, architecture, city planning, painting, drawing, advertising, typography, sculpture, Impressionism, Romantic work, modern, cubist, Japan and the Orient, fine art, architecture, printing, gold and silver.

Skoob Books
15 Sicilian Avenue, Southampton Row, Bloomsbury WC1 (0171) 404 3063
According to *Time Out* and the *Spectator*, this is the premier second-hand bookshop in London, and admittedly the shop with the palindromic name has a vast selection. A large proportion caters for students at nearby London University, so all manner of textbooks are plentiful. Downstairs are books on business, politics, history, sociology, cooking, law and militia; the ground floor houses plays, poetry, art books, biographies and the recently expanded foreign language section. Skoob Two at no. 17 has the computer science, medicine, science fiction, psychology and Far Eastern sections. Skoob also produces a limited range of its own publications, like George Eliot's poetry.

10 per cent discount for NUS members.

Spread Eagle Bookshop
8 Nevada Street, Greenwich SE10 (0181) 305 1666
Entering the Spread Eagle opposite the modern Ibis Hotel is like walking into someone's old library, brushing against tables of sheet music, newspapers dating back to the mid-nineteenth century, crystal glasses, wartime magazines and pictures. Housed in a historic coaching inn, this shop deals mainly in second-hand books, arranged methodically by subject order and with a wide and absorbing choice. A small room to one side brims over with antique clothing and linen – lace petticoats, children's nightclothes, tablecloths and napkins, and a cabinet filled with ladies' small, fancy evening bags and elaborate fans. A room at the back has more general bric-à-brac, and shelves support the odd silver-plated gravy boat and vase. Everything is cheap here, but the selection is what makes it fascinating. Also, after Greenwich's mad markets, it is a serene oasis.

The Traveller's Bookshop
25 Cecil Court, Covent Garden WC2 (0171) 836 9132
This excellent travel specialist is owned by Bernard Shapero who also runs the equally excellent antiquarian travel bookshop in Holland Park. The shop has a good selection of antiquarian travel guides and travelogues; and one of the world's largest selection of Baedeckers, some in mint condition and 100 years old: ranging from £30 to £500. Other second-hand books on the ground floor include memoirs of British Colonial exploits, *National Geographic* magazines from the 1940s onwards for 60p, *Rough Guides* and *Lonely Planets* only a year old, and books from the Fifties and Sixties for £10–15. Downstairs is an excellent range of new travel guides, maps and atlases.

Travis and Emery
17 Cecil Court, Covent Garden WC2 (0171) 240 2129
This is a second-hand and anti-

quarian music book specialist, with books on every aspect of the subject. On the ground floor there are books about musical figures like Wagner, Schubert, Pavarotti and Rossini, and engravings of composers and performers. More valuable antiquarian tomes are in the locked basement. Outside you'll find classical sheet music at 25p a copy.

Upper Street Bookshop
182 Upper Street, Islington N1
(0171) 359 3785
A diverting little bookshop, with a good general selection, especially for books on art, the performing arts, gay issues, England and history. There's also a good selection on Islington's past heritage.

Village Books
17 Shrubbery Road, Streatham SW16
(0181) 677 2667
There's a small collection of antiquarian books at the back of this shop just off the high road, with second-hand novels in the front. It's all low-key, but interesting, and the small selection offered comes at reasonable prices.

Vortex Second-hand Books
139–141 Stoke Newington Church Street, Stoke Newington N16
(0171) 254 6516
Under the trendy Vortex jazz club, this fairly large bookshop devotes half of its floorspace to stationery and cards. The other half stocks an absorbing selection of second-hand volumes neatly arranged and alphabeticized, on subjects from the fine arts to militaria and literature. Paperback novels start at £1.50. Open seven days a week.

Walden Books
38 Harmood Street, Camden Town NW1
(0171) 267 8146
This bookshop is squeezed between houses on Harmood Street, off Chalk Farm Road, making it a bit out of the way. The stock is impressive – everything is overflowing from shelves, baskets and drawers, and the owner knows his stock well – he'll even keep his eye out for a specific book if you ask him to. Open Thursday to Sunday.

Watkins Books Ltd
19–21 Cecil Court, Covent Garden WC2
(0171) 836 2182
This extensive mystic and occult specialist also deals in a wide range of inspirational and 'self-discovery' literature. Downstairs is the second-hand book section, neatly categorized into such areas as homeopathy, aromatherapy, relationships, personal development, spiritual healing, cooking and diet, dreams, mystic, philosophy, ecology, mythology, astrology, Indian philosophy, Buddhism, a small amount of poetry and fiction, Christianity, Judaism, bereavement, psychic and paranormal, UFOs and hypnotism. Paperbacks from 50p, hardbacks from £3. Upstairs is an equally intriguing selection of new books, incense and cards.

Comics and magazines

Mega City
18 Inverness Street, Camden Town NW1 (0171) 485 9320
This serious shop is not for amateurs – the staggering selection of comics in plastic packets is bewildering. Sci fi, TV, adventure weeklies and monthlies from £1.50, and although most of them are new (or at least new copies from the past five years), they have a good selection of rare comics: for example, *Superman* for £10, *Flash Gordon* for £7.50, or *Green Lantern* for £60.

Vintage Magazine Shop
39–43 Brewer Street, Soho W1 (0171) 439 8525
This marvellous shop caters for film freaks. Wade through the new film posters and stills from movies upstairs and you enter a world of crackly swing playing over a PA and old magazines going back to the 1920s (*Harpers, Elle, Vogue, Modern Screen, Photoplay, Playboy* – from £2.99), newspapers (*NME, Melody Maker, New Yorker, Saturday Evening Post* – from £2.99), comics (*Beano, Dandy, Mad*), original 30x40 film posters (from £10–500), sports and motoring mags, *Radio/TV Times*, theatre programmes and playbills, original film stills (from £2.99), sheet music from the turn of the century onwards (from £2), as well as a small collection of second-hand books and annuals, videos and records. The condition of magazines and who's on the cover determine their price – a *Record Mirror* from 1962 with Cliff on the cover cost £5, any Sixties mag with the Beatles on the front would cost rather more.

CLOTHES

See also Charity Shops, Junk Shops *and* Markets

A young design student hit the headlines at Ascot 1993 for kitting herself out in clothes for less than £21 – and looking right at home among the gentry. Gone are the days when wearing a second-hand garment was admitting poverty – now re-using clothes is all part of the creative dressing scene, and some designers like Ralph Lauren and Donna Karan specifically hunt out antique pieces to check out the cut and hang to recreate the classic antique look. The traditional tweed-stocked shops of Covent Garden have given way to a whole new breed of second-hand clothes stores, to some stocking only American imports, from very upmarket dress agencies, right down to the grab-and-wash regime of half-price bargain basements.

WHAT TO LOOK OUT FOR

If you're buying clothes – especially from the less image-obsessed shops – look out for obvious signs of wear around collars, cuffs and knees. Also check buttons and the way they do up.

American Classics
398 King's Road, Fulham SW10 (0171) 352 2853
20 Endell Street, Covent Garden WC2 (0171) 831 1210
Two pristine and up-market vintage American clothes boutiques, with spotless men's and women's clothes from the Forties, Fifties and Sixties in a carefully cultivated casual setting. Prices reflect the excellent quality and condition of the clothes, with collectors' pieces being out of reach for any but the serious buyer. Lee jeans from £20, silk ties from £15, Hawaiian shirts from £15 and denim jackets from £40 up to £250.

Annie's Antique Clothes
10 Camden Passage, Islington N1
(0171) 359 0796
Entering this wonderful little shop on two levels is like stepping back into someone's Edwardian changing room. Women's clothes on the ground floor turn up a good selection of skirts from £15, blouses from £10, hats from £8 and dresses from £25; the men's section upstairs features tweedy jackets for around £25, white dress shirts for £8–15, wool or brocade vests for £15–30, ties for £5 and trousers from £20, with lots of dinner suits. All in excellent condition in an evocative setting.

Asahi
110 Golborne Road, Notting Hill W10
(0181) 960 7299
This is the only shop in Britain to stock original second-hand Japanese kimonos, along with contemporary

jewellery, scented candles, cards, bottles and Japanese paper parasols. The kimonos come in a stunning array of colours, shapes and sizes, and start from just £15, going up to over £200 for an elaborate number. There's a box outside with kimonos under £10 and a more up-market range at the shop at *44a Kensington Church Street, Kensington W8 (0171) 795 6299.*

Bertie Wooster
284 Fulham Road, West Kensington SW10 (0171) 352 5662
This menswear boutique sells second-hand clothes for the archetypal English gent, although it's certainly not for those who like a quick bargain. The rather preppy staff will patiently show you around the perfectly preserved collection of tweedy jackets, suits, evening dress, Henley-type outfits, caps and ties, with a fair sprinkling of designer names. You'll spot tweed jackets at £75, suits for £85–120, trousers for £40, shoes by the likes of Gucci and Lanvin from £70; scarves and ties by names like Dior for £10 and coats for £110. Bertie Wooster also stocks its own label new tweed jackets for £110.

The Best of Secondhand
42 Golders Green Road, Golders Green NW11
Everything is in perfect condition in this excellent, up-market dress agency, where smart clothes of good quality are the norm – most are designer labels. Women can choose from fancy cocktail dresses from £40 at the back of the shop, blazers for around £50, pants for £29, suits for £55, felt hats for £10; menswear is equally pristine, and you'll find well-known names like Burberry, M & S and YSL here. Silk ties at £5, suits at £55–65, dinner suits at £45, jackets at £45. Everything is dry cleaned and ironed.

Bis
41 Endell Street, Covent Garden WC2 (0171) 240 7479
Another Covent Garden trendy American fashion spot, Bis has a good range of new and old, specializing in tough streetwear and fancy hand-made vests. Denim patterned jeans go for £25, pre-loved 501s for £30, original mountain boots for £30, ninety-year-old Royal Swedish Army belts for £5, men's black leather jackets for £100, denim and fleecy jackets from £30, and some beautiful handmade waistcoats – denim, cotton or linen – for only £20. They also do a mean range of velour dresses and skirts, base hats and tops, and ex-professional shoes and boots.

The Black Tulip
2a Westbourne Terrace, Waldram Park Road, Forest Hill SE23
This small New Age shop close to Forest Hill British Rail station sells mainly period clothes and accessories from the 1930s to the 1970s. Most are women's clothes, shoes, hats and bags, and prices average £3–10 for blouses, £3–15 for day dresses, £30 for evening gowns, and £20 for cocktail dresses. In the men's line, there are solid Harris Tweed jackets from £10, dinner suits and tails from £15, jackets from £5, trousers from £5 and shirts from around £5. A bargain bin sits outside with damaged articles from 50p, and the shop also sells a range of new ethnic cards, jewellery, bedspreads and candlesticks.

Blackout II
51 Endell Street, Covent Garden WC2 (0171) 240 5006
Tucked away from the main traffic of Covent Garden, this wacky vintage clothes shop is stuffed with rails of men's and women's flamboyant day and evening wear. A large proportion of the stock has never been worn and

has sat in warehouses for years. There is a leaning towards the Sixties and Seventies, and you'll find quirky Gary Glitter-inspired platforms and ritzy spangled cocktail dresses with plenty of gold lamé, as well as hats and bags with more sequins, tassles and multi-coloured patches than you've ever dreamed of. Women's blouses and T-shirts go from £12, dresses for £19–45; men's velvet jackets for £25–39, suits from £25, shirts for £10–25. There's also a hire service available including flash clothes such as an original lurid green sequined Three Degrees dress and clumpy Bay City Rollers platforms.

John Burke and Partners
20 Pembridge Road, Notting Hill W11
(0171) 229 0862
This former antiquarian bookseller has gone over to clothes to keep up with the rest of trendy Notting Hill. Books line the walls, but it's the traditional English menswear that people come here for: brogues, bow ties, ruffles for dress shirts, wooden shoe inserts, cummerbunds, hats, striped blazers and knee-high riding boots – all the things an English gent cannot do without. You'll find waistcoasts at £23, evening tails for £65, cufflinks from £5, ties for £2 and silk cravats at £6. Some First World War naval and military apparel is also evident.

DRY CLEANERS

Dry-cleaning shops often sell off clothes that people fail to pick up. It may be a long shot to find something in your size that you actually like, but keep your eyes open every time you pass your local dry cleaners. At least you know the clothes will be clean!

Cenci Rags
31 Monmouth Street, Covent Garden
WC2 (0171) 836 1400
This small, tightly packed shop carries perfect men's and women's day wear from the Thirties to the Seventies, with plenty of tweedy material, camelhair and checks. Upstairs typically features men's casual jackets from £35, Seventies black leather jackets from £38, and Sixties wool suits at £75, women's Fifties wool jackets from £42, Fifties cashmere coats for £145 and fluffy pill box hats for around £14. Downstairs is the overflowing bargain basement, where everything unsold from upstairs ends up at half-price, crammed in skilfully by staff. Quite a bit of fossicking might turn up designer jackets for around £20 and trousers for £10.

Chloé
21 Montpelier Vale, Blackheath SE3
(0181) 318 4300
This second-hand, seconds and samples shop at the heart of Blackheath village carries a range of women's fashion a step down from the heights of *haute couture.* The owner accepts mainly French, Italian and German clothes that were originally bought from her by customers, so you can find wedding dresses, coats, suits and cocktail dresses at heavily reduced prices. When I was here, it had a Zucchero top for £39, a Daks raincoat for £89, a Harvey Nichols raincoat for £45, a Dior suit for £95, and a Stephen Marks suit for £50.

Cloud Cuckoo Land
6 Charlton Place (off Camden Passage), Islington N1 (0171) 354 3141
Cramped and filled to the brim with women's glad rags, Cloud Cuckoo Land is a riot of lacy blouses, fake fur coats, accessories, pre-worn jeans, black beaded and velvet cocktail dresses and the like. Off Islington

High Street in the heart of Islington's antiques land, it covers the period from Victorian times to the 1950s. There were fur coats at £28, a red velour dress for £25, blouses from £20, lacy tops from the Fifties at £15 upwards, a coat with fur collar for £28, jeans for £20 upwards and a fur hat for £10.

Collections
48 Totteridge Lane, Totteridge N20
(0181) 446 1229
This shop, a stone's throw from Totteridge tube station, stocks only ladies' and children's new and nearly new quality clothes, costume jewellery and bags in perfect condition. All the clothes are beautifully clean, and being in a wealthy area, the shop has its fair share of clothes with high quality designer labels – like Betty Barclay and Maison Chabaron suits, YSL blouses and the like. Girls' dresses go for around £8–15, blouses from £20 and suits from £50.

The owner is looking for clothes in A1 condition, and 50 percent of retail price goes to the customer when sold. Clothes are accepted on Mondays, Wednesdays and Fridays 10.30a.m.–12.30p.m.

Cornucopia
12 Upper Tachbrook Street, Pimlico SW1 (0171) 828 5752
One of the first shops in London specializing in period clothes, Cornucopia is a riot of theatricality, with men's and women's wear from the nineteenth century right up to the 1960s. The window is filled with hats, kid gloves, feather boas and velvet, net, lace and tulle dresses, some with sequins and feathers. You'll find gold scarves with tassles, straw hats, cocktail dresses, ball gowns, lace fans, red sequinned things and plenty of shoes. When I was there, there was a black silk evening bag for £10, a black fan at £15, a velvet stole with tassles at £40, Roland Cartier gold shoes for £15, a huge brimmed black straw hat for £25 and a plastic Thirties handbag for £75. There is a small number of men's suits, ties and scarves.

COVENT GARDEN

Head for Covent Garden for more second-hand clothes shops per square mile than anywhere else in London. Start on Monmouth Street going south, with *Cenci Rags* and its half-price cast-off basement at no. 31, *Distractions* at no. 35 for designer gear, and *Spatz* at no. 48, then keep going down Neal Street with *Sam Walker* at no. 41 for men. Cut through to *American Classics* at 20 Endell Street and *Blackout II* over the road at no. 51, before making your way down to the trendy trans-Atlantic mecca – the grab 'n' buy *Flip* at 125 Long Acre. If you've got enough energy, there's always the *Oxfam* at 23 Drury Lane.

Déjà Vu
17 Greenwich Market, Greenwich SE10
It's like stepping into an opium den when you leave the chaos of the covered marketplace and enter this incense-scented room draped with different-coloured hand-printed materials from floor to ceiling. The range of second-hand clothes is small – just three racks at the back of the shop – but the experience is so ethereal that it's worth a detour all the same. Pendants hang from the walls, joss sticks and candles are there for the taking, and perfumed oils and a

range of New Age cards can be bought or sniffed. Pre-loved leather jackets go for around £35, tweed jackets for £25, shirts at £7.50 and dresses for around £15.

Designer Sale and Exchange Shop
61d Lancaster Road, Notting Hill W11
(0171) 243 2396
This small, exclusive boutique stocks second-hand designer gear by names like Liza Bruce, Chanel, Jasper Conran, Patrick Cox, Bella Freud, Katherine Hamnett, Joseph, Flyte Ostell and Vivienne Westwood for ladies and gentlemen at a fraction of the new cost. Usually clothes are only a couple of seasons old, and they also have some seconds for the taking. I found Versace jeans at £40, a Paul Smith jacket for £98, a Joseph suit for £120, and Kenzo, Comme des Garçons and French Connection shirts from £20.

Designer Second Hand Clothes Shop
24 Hampstead High Street, Hampstead NW3
This new-ish addition to the High Street focuses on a comprehensive range of designerware, from basic French labels right up to top-class *haute couture*. The husband-and-wife-team who run this clothes agency are very choosy about what they accept (they wouldn't take on my Lanvin shoes!), but the racks of mainly women's (but also some men's and children's) clothes are all in perfect condition and generally only a few seasons old. Prices are a half to a third of what you'd expect to pay retail. Women's Alaïa dress for £150, French suits at £69–99; men's Armani and Hugo Boss suits for £119–129; children's clothes from £3.

Customers with designer items to sell can decide on a price with the owners on a sale-or-return basis. All clothes must be dry cleaned and in excellent condition.

Distractions
35 Monmouth Street, Covent Garden WC2 (0171) 240 3807
This trendy new addition to Seven Dials in Covent Garden is a new unisex clothes boutique at ground level, but descend their basement stairs and you'll find racks of nearly new designer clothes going at reduced prices. Names like Armani, Conran, Farhi, Lauren and Westwood crop up everywhere. Women's lines typically include jackets – D. Hechter for £38, YSL for £35, Mary Quant for £39 – as well as things like Gautier shorts for £40, a Susan Small dress for £49, a Nicole Fahri jumper for £40, and an Issey Miyake leather jacket for £120. There's also a rail of black, slinky and sequinned cocktail dresses, and dozens of women's hats. Men can choose from shirts like YSL for £24, Bodymap for £30, Armani for £39, or Woodhouse for £25. Then there's suits: Lanvin for £100, Armani for £275, Bruno Kirches for £80; as well as jackets: Martinique for £75, Woodhouse for £70, Givenchy for £70, and jumpers: Paul Smith for £40, Bobby Sasson for £28. The clothes are not in pristine condition and may need minor repairs, but are well worth the prices asked. They can collect by arrangement.

Dolly Diamond
51 Pembridge Road, Notting Hill W11
(0171) 792 2479
This glam clothes shop sells second-hand wear a cut above the average, including vintage men's and women's clothes from the Thirties to the Seventies in really excellent condition. You'll find dinky hats with little veils, cocktail dresses, satin shoes, evening gloves, silk cravats, and men's collars, giving the place an authentic House of Eliot feel. It also sells women's antique costume jewellery, and had some beautiful

diamanté brooches from £38, Fifties enamel bracelets, a gold compact £15, gold Stardust high heeled sandals £30, feather boas and straw boaters, and a tendency towards the theatrical with black glass beads, a black beaded crochet purse for £15, glittery evening gloves, a striped grandad shirt £15, a Hugo Boss shirt for £22, a Next shirt for £15, black tailcoats from £65 up, wool and silk men's vests for £22 and a trilby for £25.

Dynasty
12a Turnham Green Terrace, Chiswick W4 (0181) 995 3846
This duo of clothes agencies sit side by side close to Turnham Green tube station, both selling top quality clothes, often with designer labels. The women's clothes agency featured things like a pink Panton two-piece wool suit for £79, a Jaeger brown wool suit for a very reasonable £69, an Escada check suit at £140 and a striking Karl Lagerfeld yellow coat for £79.

12 Turnham Green Terrace, Chiswick W4 (0181) 994 4450
The male counterpart has a range of low-brow designer clothes, clean and in perfect condition, with a range of silk, wool or leather jackets, shirts, shoes, silk ties, casual wear and suits (especially size 42 and up). I found a black leather jacket at £89, tweed suits for £40, black Bally shoes at only £25, a houndstooth jacket for £49, suede shoes for £29, Van Heusen shirts from £5 and M & S jackets from £35.

Clothes are only taken in for sale on Wednesday or by appointment.

The Emporium
330 Creek Road, Greenwich SE10 (0181) 305 1670
Around the corner from the main Greenwich one-way system, the windows of this extensive shop look remarkably like a Merchant-Ivory set. In fact, the shop rents a lot to film and television companies. The clothes here tend to be in very good condition, displayed carefully, with little theatrical flourishes, such as a display cabinet full of wacky bugle-beaded evening bags, long satin gloves and dress jewellery. The Thirties and Sixties are the most popular periods. The owner imports clothes from all over the world, so there are denim jackets for £10, leather jackets for £80, men's shirts for £12, Forties suits for £45; women's long black coats for £48, dresses for £15–30 and evening dresses from £60. At the front of the shop is also a range of chandeliers from £30 and original Thirties glass lights from £28. The Emporium also stocks some vintage clothes that are unworn and have been sitting around in warehouses for years.

Flip
125 Long Acre, Covent Garden WC2 (0171) 836 4688
A seriously hip American import shop, with excellent buys in unisex gear, and staff with attitude and piped US sounds lending credibility. There's rack after rack of ripped, bleached and battered 501s at £35, woollen lumberjack shirts from £10, waistcoats from £10, jackets from £45, real Hawaiian shirts for £75 and suits for £25. But it's the basement where the real bargains can be snapped up. Here you might find a man's Burberry for £20, old army dress jackets and boots, tweed and rayon jackets from £10, trousers for £3, as well as leather jackets and suede coats from £15, and denim shirts from £10. Everything is very creased as if it's just off the boat, and you may need to thread a needle, but it's all of reasonable quality, dirt cheap and sometimes quite unusual. Stock is updated several times a week.

Frock Exchange
450 Fulham Road, Fulham SW6 (0181) 381 2937
Started up by Michael Crawford's ex-wife, this élite little boutique just off Fulham Broadway has designer labels like Emporio Armani, Chanel, Nicole Farhi, Kenzo and YSL, featuring anything from blouses, shoes and two-piece woollen suits to evening dresses. Clothes are generally only a year or so old, and a fraction of the new retail price.

Glorious Clothing Company
60 Upper Street, Islington N1
(0171) 704 6312
Women's clothes and accessories from the Twenties to the Nineties are the mainstay of this outrageous emporium. Everything is striped, spangled, spotted, flowered, sequinned or otherwise flamboyant, and it gives off the feel of a theatre company's changing room. The two floors offer everything from Fifties net dresses with huge frothy skirts to wispy silk scarves, Sixties knee-high leather boots and teensy-weensy corduroy skirts. Jackets go for around £25, day dresses from £15, long dresses for £40, dress shirts for £14, shoes from £18–30 and knee-high leather boots for £45.

Hang Ups
366 Fulham Road, Fulham SW10
(0171) 376 8005
This small shop is a low-key affair. It had some quite nice women's velvet cocktail dresses for only £30, along with jeans at £20–30, a few men's suits for £30–40 and waistcoats at £28.

High Society
46 Cross Street, Islington N1
(0171) 226 6863
The men's and women's mainly Fifties and Sixties clothes are all in perfect condition. Vintage jeans are £30, tweed jackets £25, evening jackets £30, tail coats £70, brocade and wool vests £25, white shirts £20–30, suits £60–70, women's cotton day dresses £25 upwards, evening dresses upwards of £50, new shoes and boots £50–70. It isn't the cheapest place in town but the clothes they have are beautifully maintained and some of the waistcoats are very unusual. Sift through the £5 bargain rail while you're here.

Irene's Nearly New Gear
101 Newington Green, Stoke Newington N16 (0171) 226 2345
This small basic shop tucked out of the way from the closest British Rail station and the tube sells cheap, clean clothes for men and women, not designer fashion or trendy gear, but at prices comparable to a very reasonable charity shop. You might snap up Irene's T-shirts here for only £3, women's lightweight jumpers at £8, skirts for around £4, a woman's L'Ultima top and skirt for £10, slippers for £1, and things like men's denim shorts for £2 and jackets at just £8.

Just a Second
174 High Street, Penge SE20
(0181) 778 8794
Pristine second-hand clothes for men and women are the mainstay of this shop, down from the main crossroads in Penge and a real surprise for the south-east London suburbs. Everything here is clean and ironed and in perfect condition. Women can choose from blouses for £6.95–14.95, shirts at around £4.50, shoes for £9.75 and waistcoats for £4.50. Menswear features two-piece suits for £39.50, jackets at £16.95, trousers going for £7.95, jeans at £6.95, and shirts for £4.50. They have a few other items like costume jewellery, perfume bottles, ornaments and plates. Open Thursdays, Fridays and Saturdays.

Lipman & Sons
22 Charing Cross Road, Covent Garden WC2 (0171) 240 2310
Essentially a men's clothes hire store with an emphasis on evening dress and morning suits that sells off ex-hire gear at reasonable prices. There seems to be a permanent sale box around the corner in Cecil Court, with shirts and waistcoats from the catering industry and dress trousers going for a song. Former hire jackets in the window start at £29.95, tweed jackets at £45, pure wool day suits at £99.95, morning suits for £99, and cashmere and wool coats for £125. Also new trilbys, braces, cufflinks and cummerbunds. Not the cheapest place in town, but reliable and of good quality, and excellent for white shirts from the catering trade. Hire prices start at £9.95 for a top hat and £19.95 for a single breasted suit. Open seven days a week.

Lost City
73 Camberwell Church Street, Camberwell SE5 (0171) 708 3654
This rather inconveniently located (a no. 12 bus ride from Camberwell Green) small shop sells a weird and wonderful selection of second-hand goodies – mainly men's and women's clothes but with the odd pipe or necklace thrown in for good measure. Clothes mainly date from the Twenties to the Sixties, and are in mixed condition and of variable quality. Searching turned up a men's Jaeger jacket in need of a sewing job for £5 and some ladies' woollen trousers for only £3.

Merchant of Europe
232 Portobello Road, Notting Hill W11 (0171) 221 4203
This funky vintage clothes shop stocks items from the Fifties onwards (with the odd Victorian creation), and has a good range of the wearable and the outlandish for that Ab Fab fancy-dress party. Men's Sixties suede jackets go for around £50, shirts for around £10, and cotton and wool jackets for between £30 and £40. Long dressing gowns are about £20, striped jeans £25, ladies' Seventies trousers £20, Seventies shirts £10–15, Sixties print tops and long dresses around £15. There are more flamboyant ladies' evening wear and feather boas for hire, as well as quite a few psychedelic Sixties and Seventies outfits, kaftans and the odd outrageous bodysuit.

Ewa Minkina
164 Fortis Green Road, Muswell Hill N10 (0181) 883 0408
The owner of this second-hand women's clothes shop is an experienced tailoress who has a good eye for quality and cut, so the clothes she stocks are of high quality but also surprisingly cheap, and once inside her shop you get her undivided attention. Satin, cotton or appliqué evening dresses go from £50, woollen coats from £30 and tailored woollen jackets from £30. She also makes up clothes from owners' fabrics (bridal, evening, casual, suede and leather wear), does tailored alterations, and sells new ready-made dresses and skirts.

Second-hand clothes are accepted for sale purely on a sale-or-return basis, and must be of good quality and style, and dry cleaned.

Not Quite New
159 Brent Street, Hendon NW4 (0181) 203 4691
Posh-looking women's clothes shop at the hub of Hendon's shopping area. The shop sells a lot of dressy outfits, not average grunge clothes – your mother would definitely approve. Dresses start at around £10 and go up to £45, depending on label and age; there are trouser suits for around £20, blazers for £25, knitted tops for

around £30 and skirts at £10. The clothes are in excellent condition, and you find names like Excell, Seye Karela and Bruno Magli here.

The Observatory

20 Greenwich Church Street, Greenwich SE10 (0181) 305 1998

This trendy and typically crowded men's and women's outfitters is in a long thin shop packed with Greenwich market devotees. Racks of a good selection of well-kept (and freshly dry-cleaned) men's and women's clothes from the Twenties to the Seventies line the walls downstairs, with shirts from £7.50, cashmere pullovers from £17.50, coats from £20, 501s from £25, hats for £10 and scarves for £1. Upstairs is more formal attire, with evening suits for £39.50, tweed jackets from £20, evening dresses from £35 and velvet capes for £15.

Orsini

284 Portobello Road, Notting Hill W10 (0181) 968 1220

Fifties and Sixties dresses are the mainstay of this shop, with feathered, sequinned, velvet and floral numbers for day and evening wear starting at £20, and cocktail dresses going for around £45. Shoes start at just £2, and they have a good collection; there are also hats, camisoles, Victorian underwear and accessories, and a box outside with cast-offs for just £1.

Past Caring

76 Essex Road, Islington N1

The jovial women who run this shop have assembled racks of clothes mainly from the Thirties to the Fifties. There are men's suits for £15, tweed jackets for £10 and silk scarves for £10; women's costume jewellery from £1, dresses for £15, blouses for £5, evening dresses – often flamboyant, beaded or velvet – from £25, and oddments like a brown glazed Fifties coffee pot for £8, tea and coffee pots, jugs and sugar bowls for £10, or paperbacks from 50p.

Retro

34 Pembridge Road, Notting Hill W11 (0171) 792 1715

Part of the huge Notting Hill-based Exchange chain, Retro is a really cool, cheap, grab-bag type of shop. The men's and women's clothes here are a real mish-mash quality-wise, and may be damaged or just heavily worn – perfect for grunge freaks. Jumpers, shirts and blouses start at £3, jackets from £5, winter coats from £15 and shoes from a mere £5.

Ribbons and Taylor

157 Stoke Newington Church Street, Stoke Newington N16 (0171) 254 4735

A comfortable little shop with a good range of pre-used jeans for £9.50–20, suede skirts for £12, leather jackets for £10–30, silk-look dressing gowns at around £16, vests at £10 and plain white shirts for £9–15.

Sam Walker

41 Neal Street, Covent Garden WC2 (0171) 240 7800

Well-established top-quality men's clothes store with plenty of impeccable tweeds and corduroy from the Forties and Fifties for the classic English look. Upstairs are tweed, herringbone and houndstooth jackets from £35, new leather jackets and college scarves. Vintage watches start at £35, and enamelled cufflinks around the same. Pricier than the average, but excellent quality in perfect condition. Downstairs you'll find more formal attire, with silk ties for £10 (three for £25), tuxedos for £49, waistcoats for £35, silk scarves for £20, trilbys for £20 and suits for £100. The shop also stocks new shoes in old styles, and new socks, braces and cufflinks in classic styles.

Second Review
74 Norwood High Street, West Norwood SE27 (0181) 766 6545
This small designer dress agency stocks only women's clothes in pristine, dry-cleaned condition and features names like Bellino, In Wear, Pied-à-terre, Suzie Q and Zygo at a fraction of their original cost. It also stocks some accessories and children's wear.

Spatz
48 Monmouth Street, Covent Garden WC2 (0171) 379 0703
Voted as having some of the best vintage clothes in London by *Time Out*, this fine antique clothes and lace shop specializes in Forties and Fifties women's day wear, but also carries Victorian lace-trimmed nightgowns, some Twenties and Thirties womenswear and a range of men's tweed jackets, waistcoasts and crisp cotton shirts. Items in the shop are astoundingly pristine – antique cotton and lace apparently not only last longer, but also look fresher and newer than modern counterparts. Men's tweed jackets go for around £35, silk scarves for £8–15, waistcoats for £15 and white shirts for £25 up. The owner says that people like Donna Karan and Ralph Lauren shop here to reproduce the lines in their collections. They also sell antique bedlinen, with prices for an antique pillow and pillowcase with lace border varying from £20 to £40.

Steppin' Out
115 Kentish Town Road, Kentish Town NW5
This no-frills shop is on a tatty block on the main road going down to Camden Town and just a bit too far from the tube station to be swamped with customers. The shop is small, but stocks a good range of high street labels in nearly new women's clothes, shoes and handbags, generally only a few years old at most. Prices tend to reflect the quality and style of the item, but typically you'll find skirts here for around £8, suits for £12–15, blouses for £8–10, and shoes for £8–10.

T-Bird Classic American Clothing
166 Stoke Newington Church Street, Stoke Newington N16 (0171) 226 2777
A trendy US import shop with an all-American range of brightly coloured baseball jackets and hats, sheepskin coats, bugle beaded dresses, denim jackets and Hawaiian shirts. 501s go for £15–30, baseball jackets for £30, Hawaiian shirts for £10, suits for £20, jackets for £15, denim jackets for £30 and dresses for £15–20.

Thaddeus
329 Upper Richmond Road West, Mortlake SW14 (0181) 878 1803
A quiet dress agency, Thaddeus is run by a fastidious lady who insists on newly dry-cleaned and ironed clothes. She stocks a wide range, from High Street brand names to some designer gear and Sixties psychedelic fashion for women, and prices fall typically between £2.99 and £200. M & S blouses go for around £6, skirts for £9.99 and shoes from £5. I saw a Nicole Farhi silk dress for £50, a Jaeger wool suit for £69, Roland Cartier black suede shoes with gold tips for £20 and a Sixties psychedelic dress for £15.99.

All clothes must be dry-cleaned or pressed before they are brought in for sale. Clothes are held for one month on a sale-or-return basis, and owners receive 50 percent of the selling price.

Children's clothes

Encore
53 Stoke Newington Church Street, Stoke Newington N16 (0171) 254 5329
A friendly little shop specializing in

children's clothing and equipment in good, clean condition. The two chatty women who run Encore (along with their family members who always seem to be here) stock anything of use to mothers and children up to ten years. The clothes they sell tend to be fun, everyday items, with the odd posh item thrown in. You'll find well-known quality brand names like Gap, Hennes, M & S, Next and some foreign names like Osh Kosh, and the clothes range from 20p for a pair of socks to around £7 for a dress or coat. Baby equipment includes folding prams for £25–125, pushchairs at around £12, baby seats and appropriate books. The walls are decorated with exotic items sent from all over the world by grateful holidaying customers.

The Little Trading Company

Bedford Corner, 7 The Avenue, Chiswick W4 (0181) 742 3152

A tidy little shop up from Turnham Green tube station on the monied Bedford Park estate. The children's wear in this shop is of good quality and very well cared for, and you'll find a mixture of clothes, shoes, toys, prams, the odd video, books and jigsaws. Typical finds include a grey woollen coat (4 yrs) for £20, Dr Martens (2 yrs) for £10, shoes (1 yr) for £5, dresses from £8, and winter shirts for around £8. Open until 7p.m. on Thursday.

Skidaddle

174 Stoke Newington Church Street, Stoke Newington N16 (0171) 923 4701

A children's shop selling second-hand clothes for up to eight-year-olds, as well as new toys, puzzles, pencils, marbles and the like. The clothes are bright, colourful and inexpensive, and you'll find things like T-shirts for £2, dresses for around £3, shirts for £2.50, jackets for £8, sloppy Joes for about £2 and denim overalls for £3.50.

Winkie Jane

184 Munster Road, Fulham SW6 (0171) 384 1762

This shop is most easily accessible by car, as the nearest tube station is Parsons Green from which it is a fifteen-minute walk. If you do manage to get here, you'll find cast-offs in nearly new condition and of good quality, this being Fulham. They had denim overalls for £15, brightly coloured T-shirts from £2, more dressy dresses with lace collars for £15, jeans from £10, shorts from £5 and blue and white cotton dungarees for £14.50.

COLLECTIBLES

Some second-hand shops deal in one thing specifically – stamps, posters and engravings, china, carpets, naval and military paraphernalia, Art Deco objets d'art, *lighting or bicycles. These shops tend to have a higher quality merchandise and generally higher prices than more general shops, but their stock is more comprehensive and often in better condition. Whether you're a philatelist, crystal collector or air-gun enthusiast, there are specific outlets in London dealing with your own peculiar passion.*

A. and R. Cycles
48 Lee High Road, Lewisham SE13
(0181) 297 2465
This bicycle shop stocks a range of second-hand cycles outside on the pavement with a sign saying that no reasonable offer is refused. They tend to be mainly children's bikes, small mountain bikes or toddler's two-wheelers. From around £35.

Simon Andrews
6 Cecil Court, Covent Garden WC2
(0171) 240 1051
There's been a stamp dealer on this spot for years, and Simon Andrews carries on the tradition with an excellent worldwide collection, including stamps from Indian provinces, and handy signs in the window telling you what's in stock at the moment. There's plenty for the beginner as well, with grab bags from £7.50, 111 different football stamps for £9.95, or a couple of hundred stamps with a kid's album for just £17.50. And a few interesting items like American civil war propaganda envelopes for £12.50 and letters dating back hundreds of years on handmade paper. It also organizes postal history auctions, with the emphasis on hand-illustrated covers.

Antiques at Sheen
327 Upper Richmond Road West, Mortlake SW14 (0181) 876 4062
A new little shop shared by seven traders from the now closed Duke's Yard in Richmond, this is the friendliest, liveliest antiques shop I've ever come across, and if you come at the right time, they'll give you a glass of wine or a cup of tea. The merchandise is equally interesting, with each dealer having his or her own speciality from jewellery, rugs and Clarice Cliff pottery to silverware and decorative items, with plenty of small, unusual pieces that won't stretch your credit too far. An 1876 handpainted Worcester plate was going for around £33, a Georgian cut-glass sherry decanter for £15, an 1864 moulded jug for £38, women's summer hats trimmed with flowers for £20, a goldplated 1890 lorgnette for £60, a large Victorian jet pendant for £85, and a carved wooden gilt wall candelabra for £15.

A.H. Baldwin and Sons
11 Adelphi Terrace, WC2
(0171) 930 6879
Tucked away off Adam Street by Charing Cross station, this coin dealers – or numismatist to the initiated – is a bit Fort Knox-like and rather in-

timidating, but has a very well regarded collection of coins, banknotes and medals from all corners of the world.

Leo Baresh Ltd
110 St Martin's Lane, Covent Garden WC2 (0171) 240 1963
'Stamps of the world' is the motto of this small shop. Their stock includes a variety of first-day covers, mint and used issues and decorative packs, and they offer expert help and advice. They specialize in Austria, Switz erland and Liechtenstein, with good collections of British and Commonwealth issues. There is a very good sale once a year.

Bits and Pieces
24a The Green, Winchmore Hill N21 (0181) 886 3044
A pretty little shop filled with china and crystal from a few pounds to hundreds. The quality and age of everything here varies, but the condition is good of the jugs, china plates, huge china bowls begging for pot pourri, crystal and glassware, teapots, butter dishes and the like. Decanters go from £35; odd glasses from £1 each and a set of four was £7.50.

Blunderbuss Antiques
29 Thayer Street, Marylebone W1 (0171) 486 2444
Just up from Oxford Street, this military and maritime specialist sells a range of helmets, armour plates, rifles, hats and uniforms, all restored and gleaming. Peaked hats start at £55, hard hats as worn in the colonies at £120.

Alan Brett
24 Cecil Court, Covent Garden WC2 (0171) 836 2222
This wonderful old shop features a quirky range of goodies, such as old photos of stars, maps, acts of Parliament and the odd book. Signed photos go for various prices, depending on the popularity of the subject: Mario Lanza was £250, Chaplin £150, Alan Ladd £55, and they have original prints of people like Oscar Wilde (£300), Churchill (£450), and Wagner (£300). Original eighteenth- and nineteenth-century acts of Parliament start at £5, antique maps from £4, and general lithographic prints from £1. Six volumes of leather-bound *Old and New London* for £140.

Chelsea Bric-à-Brac Shop
16 Hartfield Road, Wimbledon SW19 (0181) 946 6894
This little shop just off the main road has some beautiful collectable pieces – Chinese plates and ornaments, china lamps with fringed lampshades, mirrors, silverware, beautiful chandeliers, finely carved chairs, trunks, china and glassware from the Twenties and Thirties, and walking sticks and books at the back of the shop. Everything is in perfect condition and beautifully presented. You must ring the bell to get in.

The Clock Emporium
184 Tottenham Court Road, Bloomsbury W1 (0171) 580 6060
The second-hand and antique clocks in the basement of this swanky clock shop tick madly away – and don't visit around midday, when the sound is so cacophonous that the Swiss Centre's clock will seem as sweet as a Carpenters' tune. There were plenty of characterful clocks ranging from a humble Sixties Imbet desk clock at £115, a wooden 1915 mantel clock or a low-key alabaster model for £210 right up to over-the-top gold ormulu and bronzed monstrosities at £1089, carved Black Forest wall clocks from the 1830s at around £925 and a range of delicious

grandfather clocks, including a walnut and olive one at a whopping £7500. Upstairs are more moderately priced new clocks, like a simple plastic kitchen clock at £17.

Coincraft
45 Great Russell Street, Bloomsbury WC1 (0171) 636 1188
A serious coin specialist opposite the British Museum, dealing in such rarities as Roman and Greek coins, banknotes from all over the world, medallions and the odd antiquity. You'll find such things as a Henry VI silver groat at £49.50, a William and Mary half-crown at £59.50, a Henry III silver penny at £34.50, ancient Greek coins from £15, a 1696 William III sixpence at £35, or an Elizabeth I sixpence at £65. They also publish *The Phoenix*, a free newspaper giving pictures and prices of their stock.

Covent Garden Oriental Carpets
20 Earlham Street, Covent Garden WC2 (0171) 240 3032
In the middle of a daily flower market is this fine rug shop that sells women's handbags made from nineteenth- and early twentieth-century Turkish carpets for £15–20, with a stall outside to entice carpetbaggers. The rugs on sale vary in size and price, and start from around £100 for a 3x5ft kilim, with some dating back to the Fifties, Thirties and further.

Covent Garden Stamp Shop
28 Bedfordbury, Covent Garden WC2 (0171) 379 1448
Rowan S. Baker has recently moved from Leo Baresh in St Martin's Lane to these premises just off New Row behind the Coliseum. His shop is perfect for beginners, away from the high-tech horrors of some of the bigger philatelists, with just one counter to approach. Admittedly you can't browse here as there is nothing on show and you must approach an assistant, but staff are helpful. They sell grab bags of 500 UK or international stamps.

Deco Inspired
67 Monmouth Street, Covent Garden WC2 (0171) 240 5719
The owners of this chi-chi shop import furniture and usable accessories from America – anything falling between Twenties chic and Fifties kitsch, hence the eye-popping collection of Formica and vinyl dinette suites, cocktail bars, black dressing tables and smaller items like jewellery, lighters, glassware and lamps. They also are Coca-Cola advertising specialists and carry trays, signs and small ads. There is an emphasis on the practical here, and so you'll find Fifties cobalt cocktails sets for £280, lamps from £70, Thirties mirrors from £250. The colours are bright and fun, the quality is high and it's like a set from *Happy Days*. The Forties and Fifties designer jewellery is all signed and mainly copper. The owner can obtain jukeboxes in mint condition, Forties typewriters and Fifties pay phones, all work and are restored. The owner also makes gilt mirrors in Art Deco style to order.

The Delightful Muddle
11 Upper Tachbrook Street, Pimlico SW1
Bric-à-brac including glassware, china, pottery and the like are the main feature in this little shop. They had ornaments from £2 in the form of dogs, birds, monk salt and pepper shakers, a china butter dish for £5.50, crystal bell £5.50, lots of glasses and plates in racks from £3, a few chamber pots at £15, decanters from £25 and crystal perfume bottles at £7.50.

J.A.L. Franks
7 New Oxford Street, Holborn WC1
(0171) 405 0274
This is a real find of an antique engraving shop, with a range of fascinating maps and engravings dating back as far as the seventeenth century, as well as first-day covers, postcards and cigarette cards. Mounted county, country and town maps included small maps of Bavaria (1601) for £30, the Philippine Islands (1858) for £40, London (1881) for £40 and Somerset (1627) for £35, and larger maps of Westminster (1720) for £125, Roman Britain (1695) for £75 and Dorset (1610) at £150. A framed selection of fifty cigarette cards from the Twenties was £50, and a loose collection of royalty postcards £23.

G.B. Mobilia
309 High Street, Acton W3
(0181) 972 1182
Most of the toys in this fascinating shop are new but it does sell secondhand Star Wars gear – like the Millennium Falcon starship for £15, or C3PO and Darth Vader models for £20 – as well as an absorbing range of vintage and modern model cars.

Stanley Gibbons
399 The Strand, Covent Garden WC2
(0171) 836 8444
Established in 1856, just sixteen years after the first penny black was printed, the impressive Stanley Gibbons is reputedly the largest stamp shop in the world, holding millions of stamps on the premises, as well as a royal warrant. On the ground floor is everything for the philately enthusiast – albums, books, guides, tweezers, price lists, right down to bundles of hundreds of used stamps for a few pounds – with expert service and a large number of stamp publications, including their self-published guide to British and Commonwealth stamps. You'll find envelopes dating back to the Twenties with franked stamps and spidery addresses from just a pound or so, and the more serious stamps behind the counter in dozens of books. There are no bargains here, but the staff know their product. There's also a mail order service. Upstairs is more light-hearted – but still tugging on the purse-strings: an autograph gallery, with hundreds of pictures of film, political and sports personalities autographed, framed or unframed. Mounted pictures start at £65 for an Abba, Fred Astaire, Ava Gardner, Richard Gere or Tom Hanks, and the framed and mounted ones start at around £150 and go up to the £100s or £1000s for a Janis Joplin, a President Kennedy with a signed letter, or a Queen Victoria.

Globe Typewriters
75–77 Praed Street, Paddington W2
(0171) 723 0771
This shop sells a small range of reconditioned typewriters, as well as new stationery. A Silver Reed manual was £32, a Brother Deluxe 500 £39, a Smith Corona SCM CX 380 electric £59, an Adler heavy duty £45, a Brother portable Deluxe 1613 £52, and there were some old models dating back to the Thirties displayed in the window.

Gold and Coin Exchange
16 Charing Cross Road, Covent Garden WC2 (0171) 836 0631
Coins, banknotes and medallions are what this shop deals in. There's an interesting range that can develop into a history lesson if you look long enough, including English hammered coins, ten shilling notes, commemorative coins and silver lozenges extolling the wonders of America. There were USA silver dollars from

between the years 1880 and 1930 for £12, old £5 notes for £80, a Queen Victoria 1887 jubilee set of commemorative coins at £1250 and a George VI set of three coronation gold coins at a mammoth £1675.

Grosvenor Prints
28–32 Shelton Street, Covent Garden WC2 (0171) 836 1979
A delightfully musty shop packed with a large selection of pre-1900 prints, lithographs, framed and unframed, black and white, tinted and etched. Prints start at around £5 for a humble Covent Garden scene to £2500 for a set of six dancing nymphs in gilt frames. There's everything from city scenes and architectural prints to portraits of soldiers, dogs and horses in the two large rooms, which are overflowing with pictures and huge folders where loose prints are kept with classical music playing. It's a tranquil place, even if the occasional motor bike revs up while going past. Prices do not include VAT.

Hirst Antiques
59 Pembridge Road, Notting Hill W11 (0171) 727 9364
A highly theatrical setting greets the browser: you see a four-poster bed hung with velvet and cherubs on the ground floor as soon as you walk in. Rugs, curtains, chandeliers and glass light fittings are everywhere, and wacky touches like a cow's head on the wall, velvet boudoir chairs, architectural salvage, a stuffed warthog, tapestry-covered chairs, fringing, pillars, chandeliers, curtains, armour, a fossilized whale skull are strewn about the shop's two floors. It's not a bargain centre, and the merchandise is often sold to companies who rent out to film and movie people, but you don't have to pay for the atmosphere.

Arthur Middleton
12 New Row, Covent Garden WC2 (0171) 836 7042
There's an old collection of medical, astronomical and weighing instruments in this atmospheric shop. It is the shop in London for antique scientific instruments, and you'll find an impressive selection of sextants, navigational equipment, terrestrial and celestial globes, brass telescopes on stands, half dissected Victorian models of bodies, old bottles, test tubes, magnifying glasses and the like, all deliciously gleaming. There's no pricing, however, and there's a rather offputting sign on the door stating 'Serious enquiries welcome: we regret no just looking.'

Martin Murray and Colin Narbeth
20 Cecil Court, Covent Garden WC2
An interesting old shop specializing in banknotes of the world, old bonds, cigarette cards and coins, purely for decorative purposes. A 1951 £5 note was £85, an old framed Chinese bond £14.50, old £1 and £5 notes from £4, 15 footballers cigarette cards from 1909 framed for £18, 20 footballer cards from 1934 framed at £70.

Avril Noble
2 Southampton Street, Covent Garden WC2 (0171) 240 1970
The antique maps and engravings in this shop just off the Strand are fascinating, and you can spend hours poring over the late seventeenth-century views of European towns and cities, maps as far back as the sixteenth century of countries of the world and especially London, many engravings of London street scenes, some David Roberts coloured engravings for a few hundred pounds, engravings of flowers and herbs. You can find something in here for as little as £15 right up to £100s. There's no repro either.

Oddiquities
61 Waldram Park Road, Forest Hill SE23 (0181) 699 9575
This shop specializes in antique lighting, whether ceiling or free-standing, glass, crystal or metal. They're serious about it – it's one of those kind of places where you have to ring the bell and be allowed in. Every conceivable style of antique light is crammed in here – Gothic, Victorian, Art Deco – with massive chandeliers and small, plain brass ones. Overhead Victorian gas lamps (converted) start at an affordable £125, and overhead brass hanging lights from around £325. Wall lights were going for £490 for a set of five, a wooden standard lamp for £65. They also do some assorted oddments, like corner cabinets, desks, tables, hearth surrounds, and whatever else they can get their hands on. Worth travelling for.

Piermont Antiques
7 Wades Hill, Winchmore Hill N21 (0181) 886 2486
A little shop with plenty of china and glass knick-knacks, pictures, silver and crystal. There was a tray of costume jewellery starting from just £1.50, hardbound books from 50p, willow pattern plates for £7, a cut-glass pickle jar for £8 and silverplated cutlery from £1.

The Print Room
37 Museum Street, Bloomsbury WC1 (0171) 430 0159
Old and rare prints are what you'll find in this shop, just around the corner from the British Museum. They have mounted pages of *Vanity Fair* from the Twenties, London engravings for passing visitors, maps of towns, counties and countries and some hand-tinted pictures. From £20.

Regimentals
70 Essex Road, Islington N1 (0171) 359 8579
This wondrous shop stocks anything associated with war, fighting, the military, etc., and would not seem out of place forming a display in the Tower of London. The window shows off armour, confederate uniforms, rifles, a Palm Beach Deputy Sheriff leather jacket, decorated brass helmets from a few hundred years ago and German wartime uniforms. Inside are medals, guns, uniforms, Star Wars toys and the like. A Browning high-powered 8mm was £135, a Colt Sheriff revolver £125, an Incredible Hulk or Darth Vader model £18–30, a Scarlet Queen's Guard jacket £350, a decorated brass helmet £495. Note that all guns are replicas or have been deactivated.

Relcy Antiques
9 Nelson Road, Greenwich SE10 (0181) 858 2812
This gracious maritime antique shop stocks a range of very good quality antiques on two spacious floors. The theme is decidedly maritime – globes, bells, anchors, telescopes, navigational equipment, maps and maritime prints, and even tusks in huge display cases, making it more like a naval museum than a shop. There is also a selection of fine furniture, from a set of eight early Victorian dining chairs to Georgian sideboards and wine tables. Everything's very well restored and all a wee bit pricy, but the atmosphere makes it a leisurely place to stumble across that brass sextant you've always hungered for.

Risky Business
44 Church Street, Lisson Grove NW8 (0171) 724 2194
This shop specializes in what they call the 'club lounge look', offering a host of atmospheric but quite useless

decorative items. They supply props and accessories for interior design and styling, evoking a bygone age of quality and luxury, and can be commissioned to create an olde-worlde look in your own living room, if the mood takes you. They sell vintage cricket bats, trophies, painted shields, hip flasks, gun cases, rods and reels, leather suitcases and prints. A picnic basket might set you back £55, a huge Victorian globe £475, leather suitcases around £75, field boots £175 and huntin', shootin' and fishin' pictures around £50.

Sports Exchange
14 Pembridge Road, Notting Hill W11
(0171) 792 8100
The sporting equipment here runs the range from tennis racquets, bicycles, football shirts, weights, wetsuits and weight tables to roller skates and skis. Typical prices are skis £45, individual weights £6, cricket bat £40, tennis/squash racquets £5, Variflex roller skates £46, or a Narin mountain bike £350. Open daily.

Stage Door Prints
1 Cecil Court, Covent Garden WC2
(0171) 240 1683
This tiny shop specializes in stage and film postcards, signed and unsigned, as well as holding a general range of antique engravings. The bargain box outside always has a good (if slightly tatty) range of prints guaranteed to be 100 years old or more, and you can find city scenes, animals, flowers, maps and theatrical engravings from £1 ready to be mounted and framed, as well as theatre programmes starting at £1.25. Inside are postcards of stage and screen stars dating back to Victorian times in large photo albums, a fascinating selection of publicity stills, with the price varying according to the popularity or mortality of the star: £40 for a signed Liz Taylor, £40 for a signed Shirley MacLaine, £300 and over for Clark Gable or Carole Lombard, and £328 for a signed Judy Garland. Poor old Ann Miller weighed in at only £28. Black and white unsigned postcards go for £5–10.

Stamp Centre
77 Strand, Covent Garden WC2
A minuscule shop with just one desk and a lot of folders filled with stamps. It's a very small operation, but is good for beginners as it's more personal and less intimidating than a lot of the other bigger dealers. They had 1000 British Empire super starter bag for £19.95 and a 100g bag of international stamps worldwide for £4.95.

Harold T. Storey
3 Cecil Court, Covent Garden WC2
(0171) 836 7777
This print shop has a very good range of stock, with a lot of engravings and prints mounted and ready to be framed to appeal to tourists. There are plenty of maps – when I was there they had both city and country ones of mainly England, prints of flowers, fashionable Victorian scenes and naval/military scenes and a series of large David Roberts engravings of Egypt. Prices start at around £15.

Strand Stamps
79 Strand, Covent Garden WC2
(0171) 836 2579
A small shop with stamps from all over the world, across the Strand from – and very much in the wake of – Stanley Gibbons. You'll find a more modest collection here, but it's less intimidating and friendlier, but still with knowledgeable staff. There were British stamps from 25p to £1000s, a hundred mixed worldwide stamps grab bag for £1.50, a Turkey 1928

Agricultural and Industrial exhibition set of six for £70, and first day covers sit on the counter in boxes.

Tooting Exchange Centre
152–154 Upper Tooting Road, Tooting SW17 (0181) 672 6504
This threatening-looking shop has a slew of air weapons, daggers, swords, guns and knives, as well as more sedate merchandise like cameras, coins, musical instruments and stereo equipment. It stocks big names in guns like Anschultz, ASI, Sheridan, Walthar and Webley. You'll also find things like a Hitachi tuner for £25, a JVC cassette deck at £45, a Nad tuner for £40, a Kenwood cassette deck at £64 or an Olympus camera for £15. And guns like a junior Webley for £75, a 22 Webley for £115, a 177 BSA Scorpion original for £79 or a 177 mod 6 target for £68. An elaborately carved knife in a sheath was going for around £12.

Top Quality Secondhand Bike Shop
39 Essex Road, Islington N1
(0171) 704 1384
There's a reasonable array of pre-used bikes of all kinds here – mountain bikes, racers, hybrids, BMX and choppers, starting at around £40. I saw an Apollo Atomic for £75, a Raleigh impulse for £75, an Apollo Equipe for £55, an Apollo Kalamunda for £90, a Hard Rock specialized for £150 and a Peugeot for £50.

Unique Collections of Greenwich
52 Greenwich Church Street, Greenwich SE10 (0181) 305 0867
Right down near where the *Cutty Sark* is moored, this tiny shop specializes in things that little boys are interested in: toy soldiers, model cars such as Corgis and Dinkys in their original boxes from £10, fire helmets, police helmets, badges from £3 or sets of six tin soldiers. These are all originals in perfect condition for serious collectors.

Valantique
9 Fortis Green, East Finchley N2
(0181) 883 7651
Owner Valerie Steel has crammed in an awful lot over two floors of this lighting and fender specialist shop just off East Finchley High Road. Outside are chained a series of larger pieces like a Victorian dining chair (£130), umbrella stand (£85) or wine table (£75). Inside on the ground floor, decorative plates like Spode, Amari and lots of blue and white line the walls, starting at £5. Display cabinets and shelves hold china, decanters, figurines and lamps, and the ceiling is invisible behind the mid-Victorian to Fifties lights hanging down: 1930s glass lights start at £40, crystal chandeliers will go for £150 and up. Up the stairs are stuffed dozens of coal scuttles, mirrors, pictures and plates, and the two rooms upstairs have a similar quantity of fenders from £90, with small tables, chairs and cabinets thrown in. A 39-piece 1905 Blyth bone china tea service was £299.

Whiteway and Waldron
305 Munster Road, Fulham SW6
(0171) 381 3195
Great for those with a religious bent, Whiteway and Waldron can kit your home out like the inside of a medieval chapel with an absorbing range of ecclesiastical Gothic bits and bobs removed from deconsecrated churches – mainly nineteenth-century ones. You might find reliquaries, statues, a bishop's gold and scarlet robe for £150, anointing bottles for £5, a lectern in brass for £150, crosses, panelling, leaded lights, an old pew for £150, bibles, pillars, doors, pulpits, brass candlesticks from £20 to £400, religious icons, stained glass from £100. Near Parsons Green tube station.

The Witch Ball
2 Cecil Court, Covent Garden WC2
(0171) 836 2922
Posters and engravings relating to the theatre, opera or ballet worlds top the bill at this chi-chi shop. Most of the works are framed, although they do have a selection of mounted antique prints inside, and you'll find posters and prints from hundreds of years back right up to the Thirties. There was an engraving of the Scala (1840) £200, a Royal Opera House programme from 1905 framed for £140, a New Orleans carnival programme from 1901, framed, for £185, mounted engravings from £5, hand coloured engraving of Covent Garden from 1870 for £75. Inside are also some books in suitably related arts fields.

Yacht Parts
99 Fulham Palace Road, Hammersmith W6 (0181) 741 9803
Mainly new yachting paraphernalia is sold here, but this marine chandlery also deals in old pumps, clocks, shackles, dinghies and some clothes. Many pieces are used for film and photographic sessions, and can make attractive, unusual ornaments. The shop also carries a range of new yachting shoes, caps, T-shirts, waterproof coats, books and jumpers.

ELECTRICAL GOODS

There are plenty of shops dotted around town that sell whites – washing machines, fridges, driers and ovens to the uninitiated – as well as second-hand stereo systems and separate components, videos and specialized things like sewing machines or even disco lighting. You can pick up whites a couple of years old and in pristine condition for around a third of what you'd pay for the things new – and you can still get a six- or twelve-month guarantee on parts and service if you shop around.

The A.C.R.E. Company Ltd
389 Green Lanes, Finsbury Park N4
(0181) 340 0171
Close to the park and Finsbury Park tube/British Rail station, A.C.R.E. displays much of its second-hand stock on the pavement outside. It has fridges, washing machines, hoovers, fans and lights, as well as new vacuum cleaners, carpet shampooers, clocks and hairdriers. Typical stock includes a Lec fridge/freezer for £85, an Electra fridge at £57, and a large Hotpoint fridge/freezer for around £95. Delivery is extra.

All Make Domestic Appliances
468 Green Street, Upton Park E7 (0181) 472 2855
Fridges, fridge/freezers, washing machines and cookers in good condition at competitive prices.

Appliance 2000
338 Balham High Road, Tooting SW17
(0181) 767 8378
Reconditioned ovens, fridges and washer/driers right next door to Tooting Bec tube station. You'll find all the merchandise in top-quality condition and with a three-month guarantee. Gas freestanding ovens from £150, Flavel gas cooker £175, Lec and Zanussi small fridges £55, Hoover, Hotpoint or Indesit washer/driers £180–225, Electra, Electrolux or Scandinavia fridge/freezers £130 upwards.

Best Refrigeration
209 Uxbridge Road, West Ealing W13
(0181) 567 5080
There's a three-month guarantee on parts and labour on all the fridges sold in this shop, and you'll find Hotpoint, Kinis, Lec and Triplex, among others. Small one-door fridges start at £45, two-door fridges from around £75.

Bobsboxes
42 Lavender Hill, Battersea SW11
(0181) 738 0705
Part of the Bobsboxes chain, this shop has fully guaranteed Finlandia, Granada and Rediffusion colour TVs from only £30 and videos from £60, alongside newer TVs with Teletext averaging at around £90. Spot cash is paid for trade-ins and you can part exchange. There's also an in-house repair service.

Also at 265 Clapham Road, Clapham SW4 (0171) 924 9971

Bobsboxes
46–50 Streatham Hill, Streatham Hill SW2 (0181) 678 1338
This large showroom features just TV

sets from £60 to £95, the upper price bracket having remote control, and with a six-month guarantee on parts and labour.

Brockley Appliances
366 Brockley Road, Brockley SE4
(0181) 691 7014
Excellent whites shop specializing in second-hand built-in ovens and hobs, with some fridges and washing machines in stock. They offer very good deals on merchandise mainly three years old and under, such as electric ovens (single and double) from £150, or washing machines at £140. Some ovens have microwaves in-built. Some ovens are ex-display models and don't have a scratch on them. There's free delivery locally, and a six-month guarantee thrown in.

Busboxes
268 Old Kent Road, Southwark SE1
(0171) 708 1243
This tiny Old Kent Road second-hand shop claims to have the lowest-priced TVs in the UK, with Finlandia, Granada and Philips models going from £30 and videos from £60. There was a special-offer TV, video and stand for just £85 when I was there. All merchandise is guaranteed for 3–12 months, and a part-exchange scheme is in operation.

Central Television Video
21a Catford Hill, Catford SE6
(0181) 314 5881
For about the cheapest TVs in London, this shop is the place to go. It's tucked away just under the railway bridge by Catford British Rail station, and sells TVs from just £15 – usually in that late Seventies/early Eighties woodgrain finish with names like Bush, Hitachi and Philips – and oddments like a stereo system in a cabinet for £20. Mainly new TVs and videos apart from that.

Chapman Sewing Machines
80 Parkway, Camden Town NW1
(0171) 267 0527
This tiny shop was founded in 1937 and has offered unbeatable deals on sewing machines, offering a three-year guarantee with each sold. Stock included an old Singer pedal sewing machine on a wooden base for £55, and vacuums starting at £35 with a one-year guarantee. They also repair anything electrical and accept trade-ins.

Clean Machines
225 Munster Road, Fulham SW6
(0171) 385 4747
For a comprehensive selection of whites, look no further than Clean Machines, a little corner shop, which had stock like a small Electra fridge for £60 (three-month guarantee), a Lec two-door fridge at £105 (three-month), a Jackson freestanding electric cooker for £169 (six-month), a Creda freestanding electric cooker at £169 (six-month), as well as Hoover and Hotpoint washing machines for £179 (three-month).

CMP Installations
23 Boston Road, Hanwell W7
(0181) 567 1778
A small whites shop, typically with goods like a Hotpoint washer/drier for £235, a small Electra fridge for £86, or a Hotpoint washer for £135.

Computer Exchange
65 Notting Hill Gate, Notting Hill W11
(0171) 243 1863
Stacked with modern computer games, keyboards, screens and the odd old fashioned typewriter for a bit of historical perspective. I saw a Prism colour monitor for £60, an electric typewriter for £35, keyboards from £20, and Amiga, Ataria and NES PC compatible games from £4. Open seven days a week.

Also at 143 Whitfield Street, W1
(0171) 916 3110

Cookerama Cookers
137 Lewisham Way, New Cross SE14
(0181) 692 6668
A shabby little shop with used electric and gas ovens with makes like Cowan, Main Aries or Parkinson, along with some fridges. There are no prices displayed, so make an offer.

CSC Electronics
329 Green Lanes, Finsbury Park N4
(0181) 880 2098
Next to Finsbury Park, this shop has a small range of reconditioned televisions, with 20-inch TVs for £75.

Dalston Sound and Lights
40a Dalston Lane, Dalston E8
(0171) 923 3846
A large shop with a wide range of music and lighting equipment, including graphic equalizers, professional DJ turntables, sampling processors, speakers, disco lights and amps. Typically you'll find equipment like a Nad tape deck for £65, an Echo chamber for £75, a Yamaha mixer M206 for £70, or a Mitsubishi stereo cassette for £45.

Discount Domestics
731 High Road, Leytonstone E11 (0181) 539 1636
Whites galore, with a six-month guarantee on most of the second-hand items that pass through here. You'll typically find a large Tricity two-door fridge/freezer for £110, a large Hotpoint fridge/freezer for £145, a Hotpoint washer/drier for £225, a Hotpoint washing machine at £165, or freestanding electric Creda ovens from £145.

Domestic Appliance Service Centre
4 Winchmore Hill Road, Southgate N14
(0181) 886 8050
An excellent little shop that has a good range of reconditioned and guaranteed cookers, refrigerators and washing machines, like a Zanussi washer/drier for £275 (six-month guarantee) or £300 (twelve-month guarantee), an Electrolux small freezer for £120 (six-month guarantee) or £140 (twelve-month guarantee), a Tricity Princess cooker at £180 (six-month guarantee) or £200 (twelve-month guarantee), and a large Lec fridge/freezer for £140 (six-month guarantee only).

Domestic Appliances
553 Green Lanes, Finsbury Park N4
(0181) 342 8988
Housing Association and DSS cheques are accepted in this little corner shop that stocks reconditioned appliances like Hotpoint washer/driers for £195, washing machines for £135, a Baby Belling oven for £80, a Teka built-in oven £225, an Electra large fridge/ freezer at £110, a Thorn strata freestanding oven for £115, or a small Tricity Triumph fridge for £60.

East London Cooker Centre
171 Morning Lane, South Hackney E9
(0181) 981 8266
The usual array of gas and electric cookers, washing machines, fridges and tumble driers, all fully serviced and guaranteed, with free fitting and delivery. They had a Belling Compact 3, a Belling Classic, Hotpoint washer/driers, fridges both one- and two-door, and gas heaters.

FJS Gas
2–4 The Broadway, Crouch End N8
(0181) 348 8308
This shop has been selling electrical goods from here for ten years, and deals exclusively in fridges, freezers, ovens and washing machines, mainly of English manufacture. All appliances have been overhauled, and delivery and installation are included

in the price. Fridge/freezers, ovens and washing machines all go for £120–220, washer/driers for about £220 and freezers for £60–145.

Gas Cookers
390 Caledonian Road, Holloway N7
(0171) 607 1004
A little electrical appliance shop stocking things like a New World Tempo for £145, a Valor Bistro for £120, a Parkinson Cowan for £135, or a Newhome Corvette for £110. Not open on Saturdays.

J.J. Goddard
387 Hackney Road, Bethnal Green E2
(0171) 739 7729
Close to Cambridge Heath British Rail station, this shop specializes in gas appliances and is a registered Corgi dealer and gas appliance installer. Typical second-hand merchandise includes a gas Leisure 5 star Auto Mk II freestanding cooker for £155, a New World Nova for £155, or a small Flavel Vaness at £90, along with a range of gas fires. You'll also find the odd electrical item, like a freestanding Creda cooker for £155, including delivery and fitting.

Gogglebox
239 Walworth Road, Walworth SE17
(0171) 252 0774
This shop – down from the Elephant and Castle on any of the numerous buses – sells reconditioned Ferguson, Finlandia, Hitachi, Pye, Sharp and Visionhire television sets from £65, with Teletext models from £95; videos start at £95 as well, many with a one-year guarantee.

Granada
139 Edgware Road, Paddington W2
(0171) 723 7853
A good TV outlet, selling ex-rental TVs that have been reconditioned and fully tested, and come with a three-month warranty. Colour TVs feature names like Finlandia, Granada, Hitachi and Philips, selling for about £79–99, and TVs with Teletext for around £120.

Halcyon Electronics
423 Kingston Road, Wimbledon Chase SW19 (0181) 542 6383
Only the electronically initiated will benefit from this shop, which sells a mentally challenging array of generators, gauges, surveillance monitors, rectifiers and multi-indicators. An HW Sullivan variable capacitor D-1100 was £35, a Xenon flash units £19, a Dragon colour computer £25, a Racal Oscilloscope £149.

Home Appliances
98 Cricklewood Broadway, Cricklewood NW2 (0181) 208 1225
Home Appliances sells a range of reconditioned appliances at sensible prices, with a three- or six-month guarantee. A Frigidaire fridge/freezer goes for around £75, a Hoover washing machine for £125, a Hotpoint washer/drier for £250. Includes delivery.

LMM Supermarket
241–243 High Street, Acton W3
(0181) 993 4588
A small supermarket with a shop selling reconditioned electrical goods attached – Electrolux vacuums go for £59, an Indesit washer/drier for £95, a Creda electric oven at £139, a New World gas oven for £125, and a Lec fridge/ freezer at £120.

Lordship Cooker Centre
447 Lordship Lane, Tottenham N17
(0181) 889 4350
The reconditioned gas and electric cookers, water heaters and fires sold in this large showroom are all guar-

anteed; there are also some new washer/driers and freestanding cookers, and a Parkinson Cowan tumble drier was £179. Otherwise, the goods here are mostly new stock.

Market TV

267 Portobello Road, Notting Hill W11
(0171) 229 8801
A little shop with new and used electrical goods, like reconditioned colour TVs from £25 and black-and-whites from £15. Teletext TVs start at £85. They also have a wide range of new blank video tapes, head cleaners, cassette tapes, headphones and new CD players and cassette decks.

Micro TV

89 Tottenham Lane, Hornsey N8
(0181) 348 2030
Remote control TVs start at £95, and videos at £89.

New Cross Appliances

453 New Cross Road, New Cross SE14
(0181) 634 1154
This rough-and-ready shop on the A2 sells a range of reconditioned household appliances at reasonable prices. Upright fridge/freezers with makes like Hotpoint or Lec start at £99, washer/driers with makes like Hoover and Hotpoint start at £160, electric ovens from £95 and gas ovens from £85. There are also various new bits and pieces.

Ovaltronics

244 Kennington Park Road, Kennington SE11 (0171) 582 5923
A little electronic shop, Ovaltronics deals in stereo components, TVs, videos and radios at good prices. A Ferguson black-and-white 14-inch set was going for £38, a Sony digital CD for £75, a Rotel stereo receiver £59, a Toshiba CD £95, and speakers for £17.99.

Plaza Appliances

170 Harrow Road, Willesden NW10
(0181) 838 2734
Tucked away around a corner from the main shops in Willesden, Plaza Appliances sells fully reconditioned washing machines, washer/driers, fridges and ovens at reasonable prices.

The Recon Shop

7 High Street, Penge SE20
(0181) 778 1977
This TV and whites shop sells colour sets from £35, remote control TVs from £60, and TVs with Teletext from £75. Videos start at £80. Whites like a Hoover 1300 washer/drier with six-month guarantee go for £199, a small Philips freezer for £70, freestanding ovens from £200, and a two-month old pristine Philips Whirlpool built-in oven £285, with a six-month guarantee.

Sam's TV

145 Bethnal Green Road, Bethnal Green E2 (0171) 613 2338
Sam stocks colour TVs from £45 – Baird, Ferguson, Philips and Toshiba mainly – and videos for £65–125; there are also other oddments like stereos and studio mixers for the taking.

Second Time Around

406 Green Lanes, Palmers Lane N13
(0181) 882 8255
On the corner of Windsor Road is this small shop that reconditions and sells second-hand washing machines, driers, ovens, vacuum cleaners and fridges. Hoover, Hotpoint and Zanussi washing machines start at £80, fridge/freezers and tumble driers from £50, Belling and Electrolux upright electric ovens from £80. There was an NEI fridge for £40 and a Goblin classic vacuum cleaner for £20.

Sewcraft
150 King Street, Hammersmith W6
(0181) 745 0808
This specialist shop sells new and second-hand sewing machines, the reconditioned models starting from £45. Typically, you'll find a Viking at £74.95, a Chivoda at £69, a Seamstress at £69, an old Sherwood at £39, a New Home with buttonholer and embroidery function at £139, an almost new Suger with buttonholing programme at £109, sitting right next to a high-tech new microchip compute rized machine at a whopping £1399. Most of the sewing machines come with three-year guarantees.

Stereovision
64 Green Lanes, Stoke Newington N16
(0171) 254 8052
A little shop with TVs from £49 and videos from £100; typically, you'll find sets like a Ferguson with remote control for £119, a Toshiba Blackstripe at £94.99, or a Grundig SuperColour for £79.99.

Stratton Brothers
201a Belsize Road, Kilburn NW6
(0171) 624 0175
This small outlet sells well-maintained reconditioned gas appliances, fridge/freezers, water heaters and ovens, which, with grill and guarantee, go for £159 and up. A Valor Corvette oven was £185.

Studio SAV
17 Bell Street, Marylebone NW1
(0171) 258 3448
A shop selling electronic gear for professional musicians and sound people as well as photographers. Old gramophones, radios and telephones exhaust the historical side of the stock, but I saw newer equipment including a Toa double-play cassette deck for £135, a Hitachi tube camcorder for £580, a Panasonic state colour camera for £265, pro metal tool box £75, a Sony timer unit with charger for £235, a Sony multi system tuner for £359, and a Sony 5850 edit-rec for £1899.

Supertel
478–486 Old Kent Road, Southwark SE1
(0171) 232 0547
This is a cash-and-carry outlet of Granada which sells off ex-rental TVs and videos at greatly reduced prices, with guarantees of 3–12 months depending on age. Models include Finlandia, Panasonic, Philips, Sharp and Toshiba. Most models are around two years old. TVs start at £50 and go up to £300; videos range from £75 to £229.

Chris Tantelli
409 Green Lanes, Finsbury Park N4
(0181) 341 3585
A sewing-machine repair shop that stocks a small array of reconditioned trade-in models, like a Singer Styliste for under £110 or a Singer 507 for £117.50.

Tel Boys
5 Mile End Road, Bow E1
(0171) 702 8277
A small shop selling mainly white goods like a Hotpoint drier for £75, a Philips washing machine for £150, a Hotpoint washer/drier for £220, as well as a few pieces of furniture like a TV or wardrobe.

Tokyo Electrics
117 Fulham Palace Road, Hammersmith W6 (0181) 748 1861
This pristine little shop is run by a Japanese woman with a keen eye for her stock, hence the good range of well-maintained ovens (both gas and electric), fridges, mircowaves and washing machines. Brand names like Hoover, Hotpoint, Indesit, Lec and Tricity proliferate, and everything is well scrubbed and comes with a

three-month guarantee and free local delivery. Ovens go from £120, fridge/freezers from £135, and microwaves from just £50.

Trading Post
485 Woolwich Road, Charlton SE7
(0181) 293 3722
This little shop is cheap – it deals in house-removal whites, and you'll typically find freestanding gas and electric ovens, washing machines and fridges. A Creda washer/drier goes for £150, a Hotpoint one for around £165; a Lec fridge/freezer was £65.

Upton Park Domestic Appliances
465 Green Street, Upton Park E7
(0181) 470 1487
New and reconditioned fridges, cookers and washing machines are what this place sells. A large Electrolux fridge/freezer was going for £125 and had a six-month guarantee.

Used Hi-fi
23 Bell Street, Marylebone NW1
A dark, noisy place with a reasonable range of new and second-hand music system equipment. Most of the second-hand stuff is amplifiers: you might typically find a Quad power amp 303 for £120, a Yamaha power amp YST-AS for £130, a Yamaha power CR-1000 receiver for £180, a Pioneer power amp 330 for £110, a QED control box for £11, a Pioneer PL-1000 amp for £150, and a Yamaha CT-610 tuner for £65.

Vincents
197–199 High Road, Willesden NW10
(0181) 459 3755
A shabby shop covering two premises and stocking a good range of reconditioned ovens, washing machines and fridges, ranging from a gas freestanding Leisure 5 star Auto Mk II to a range of single-door fridges and Electrolux, Foodcare, Lec two-door models.

X
61 Upper Street, Islington N1
(0171) 704 1124
An upbeat shop that stocks musical instruments, hi-fis, TVs, videos, photographic equipment, computers and computer games. The stock is not comprehensive, and they tend to have a little bit of everything, but the staff are very helpful. In the photographic line, you might find anything from a Fuji 35mm at £10 up to a Minolta at £175, with plenty of Hanimex, Kodak, Olympus, Pentax and nothing too expensive. An Apple Mac monitor was £180; it also had computer games, like a pack of 5 Sega mega drives for £40, or a game boy game for £12; and in the musical instrument field it had keyboards, guitars (both acoustic and electrical), clarinet £195, flute £120; hi-fi gear featured a CD/radio/tape deck £220, amplifiers, the odd tuner, a Philips radio/cassette deck for £30, and a pair of BOSF speakers for £140.

Youngs Disco Centre
20 Malden Road, Kentish Town NW5
(0171) 485 1115
Entering Youngs Disco Centre is like walking into someone's thirtieth birthday party in Tooting – it's loud, with people's skin turning green under the flashing lights and hands boosting the music volume. You'll find light boxes, amplifiers, karaoke equipment, self-operation disco equipment and lights here, either to buy or for hire.

Zam Domestic
25 Upton Park Road, Upton Park E7
(0181) 548 0002
A range of mainly gas cookers, fridges and plenty of microwave ovens, reconditioned and guaranteed.

FURNITURE

See also Junk Shops *and* Markets

There's a fine line between a rickety old piece of furniture and an antique, but even the act of incorporating 'antiques' into a shop's name seems to automatically raise prices by 50 percent. By buying second-hand, you can save quite a bit of cash, as well as having the satisfaction of renovating a hidden treasure and turning that piece of junk into heritage. There are also some antiques shops that are outstanding for their range, quality or value for money. You can find everything from that fake-wood-finish chest of drawers and wardrobes to Fifties kitsch and Victorian and Edwardian booty from these furniture shops.

139 Antiques
139 Green Lanes, Stoke Newington N16
(0171) 354 2466
This is a house removals shop with a better-than-average presentation. It has some nice pieces like a Victorian carved dressing-table mirror for only £150, a repro desk at £175 and a walnut veneer drinks table at £48, as well as some pieces of jewellery, old crockery, china and glassware.

Aladdin's Cave
146 Maple Road, Penge SE20
(0181) 643 4116
House clearance centre with heaps of old junk, especially large pieces of furniture at very low prices. There are books, bookcases, chests of drawers, tables, sideboards, cabinets and things like a nest of three perfect teak tables for £40.

Alan's Beds
58 Well Hall Road, Eltham SE9
(0181) 850 1357
This little local shop sells mainly new bedding, but also carries a modest range of cheap second-hand furniture, like wardrobes from £30, dining tables from £35, a set of four dining chairs for £25, a child's dressing table for £10, or a Hotpoint washer/drier for £95. There are also various games, glasses and chinaware.

All Furniture Bought House Clearance
216 Norwood Road, West Norwood SE27
Plenty of flat-fillers here in a no-frills showroom of wardrobes, sideboards, mattresses and tables in reasonable condition. A nest of three teak tables was £45, an almost-new two-door robe for £65, a teak wall unit in perfect condition for £95, a small battered chest of drawers for £20, a Sixties dressing table for £45 and a Fifties wardrobe for £40.

Andrew's Office Furniture
49 Fulham High Road, Fulham SW6
(0171) 610 6113
Close to Putney Bridge tube station is London's largest supplier of office furniture – new and second-hand. You'll find all manner of swivel chairs, lights, chesterfields in leather for the MD's office, filing cabinets in a

grey metal or a wood finish for the media types, and hatstands.

Also at 265a Mare Street, Hackney E8; 48 Shepherd's Bush Road, Shepherd's Bush W6.

Antique Bargain Centre

183–185 Bermondsey Street, Bermondsey SE1 (0171) 357 6007

This is a serious antique trader; prices are cheap compared with the other Bermondsey showrooms, and you'll find many pieces that end up in Islington antique shops at twice the price. On four floors are hundreds of antiques displayed, most in good condition and some unusual. I saw a William IV dining table for £790, a carved walnut dining table for £490, a carved standard lamp for £90, large framed hunting prints for £125 and a huge Thirties wardrobe for £180. The quality is high and the prices reasonable for a serious collector.

Antique Warehouse

9–14 Deptford Broadway, Deptford SE8 (0181) 691 3062

Fine quality antiques at comparatively low prices; this large shop on the main London–Dover road has a huge selection of Victorian pine with plenty of dressers, dining suites, towel rails, bedheads and trunks, and chests of drawers from £165, all in very good condition and superbly restored and treated. The other half of the showroom is devoted to very high-quality, well-treated Victorian, Georgian and Edwardian pieces, beautifully renovated and many of them large, but at lower prices than you'd pay in Islington or Notting Hill. Magnificent mahogany Victorian dressing tables start at £600, huge carved wardrobes of the same period at £1800, dining suites at £1000 and desks at £500. There is also the odd side table, chaise longue, picture or clock.

Antiques and Furniture

329 Kingston Road, Wimbledon Chase SW19 (0181) 540 0219

A down-market antiques or a good-quality house clearance shop with things like an old oak table, a barometer, pictures, repro wardrobes, old school desks, a Thirties Arts and Crafts dresser, a newish pine corner unit and pine folding chairs.

Art Furniture

158 Camden Street, Camden Town NW1 (0171) 267 4324

A peaceful furniture warehouse next to the railway line offering two spacious floors of specialist, reasonably priced Arts and Crafts, Art Nouveau, Gothic and Art Deco pieces. Most are large, in very good condition, like a Fifties three-piece Airlorn lounge suite for £480, a beautiful Thirties oak carved wardrobe for £475, a Fifties walnut veneer cocktail sideboard at £380, and there was the odd elaborately carved Victorian Gothic-style sideboard. Dining suites start at a very reasonable £300.

G. Austin & Sons

11–23 Peckham Rye, Peckham SE15 (0171) 639 3163

G. Austin is a south London institution and has been a haven trading furniture, collectibles and antiques from these premises close to the Common for years. The excellent selection of antiques and second-hand furniture over three floors is staggering. Quality and age decrease the higher up you go: the ground floor is filled with good quality, big old pieces – eighteenth-century dining suites, Victorian sofas, sideboards and wardrobes – and the top floor is a mish-mash of Sixties sideboards, Fifties sofas and the like, where you can pick up a tatty wardrobe from £35.

Nicholas Beech Antiques
787–789 Wandsworth Road, South Lambeth SW8 (0171) 720 8552
Pine furniture is the mainstay of this shop, all stripped, restored and waxed and in excellent condition. A waist-high, beautifully carved sideboard was £350, a round carved mirror £55, a large 8-foot high dresser £500, a pine bedbase with head and foot £245 and a painted sidetable £125.

Bermondsey Antique Traders
158 Bermondsey Street, Bermondsey SE1 (0171) 378 1000
This large showroom has some very nice pieces, some large and many of a very high quality, although prices may seem high. A set of fourteen George III style chairs was £2950, a George III table £2200, a Victorian mahogany triple door wardrobe £995, a huge carved rosewood chair £1175, pair of elaborate gilt armchairs, £825, a mahogany consul table £295, a Victorian mahogany chest of drawers £345. Upstairs is a floor of solid mahogany repro furniture, nicely put together. In the basement are lots of stunning large Victorian rectangular dining tables, from around £895.

Bridge Antiques
Deptford Bridge, Deptford SE8
There's a cluster of antiques and second-hand shops here on the main London–Dover road which display chairs and odd pieces along the pavement while their owners strip down tables and chests of drawers as the A2 traffic whizzes by. This shop is the next notch up from a house clearance place, and stocks mainly Thirites and Fifties pieces like wardrobes (from £65), chests of drawers (from £35) and stripped pine trunks (from £70). There's also the odd nice piece like a pine Victorian dresser for just £250.

Broadway Furniture
52 The Broadway, Crouch End N8 (0181) 340 7546
This High Street house clearance place stocks mainly modern furniture of the velour-lounge-suite variety, in very good condition and at very reasonable prices. A new-looking octagonal teak dining table and six chairs covered in spotless beige material was £425, an IKEA-style bedside table with drawers £16, a fridge/freezer £110, a wonderful old wooden trunk £165, a wardrobe £95, an electric oven £110 and a leather armchair £95.

Brockley Cross Furniture
28a Brockley Cross, Brockley SE4 (0181) 692 1153
This house-clearance place lies next to the railway line in a damp, dark Victorian building, and you really have to sift through the large pieces on offer to find anything decent. It caters for the bottom end of the market, so expect to find Seventies pine and laminated tables, wardrobes and chests of drawers, Fifties dressing tables and the odd interesting Thirties piece. No prices are shown, so bargain. Free local delivery.

Oliver Browne's
374 Brixton Road, Brixton SW2 (0181) 733 1199
The mixed selection of furniture spills out on to the pavement on the corner of Stockwell Park Road, with the cheaper merchandise stacked up – a drier for £35, cookers from £85, a bookcase for £25. Inside on three large floors are better-quality selections like Edwardian dining chairs for £20 each, a shimmering red velvet Victorian settee for just £65, a repro sideboard for £95, living-room suites for £50, and a room full of wardrobes, sideboards and dressing tables.

Brownhill Furniture Store
267 Brownhill Road, Catford SE6
(0181) 697 1100
This small local removal shop has a lot of office furniture, like filing cabinets and office desks, as well as household bits and pieces. You'll typically find a TV for £55, a small 1930s chest for £20, wardrobes from around £65 and an almost-new built-in oven for £160.

Butlers Furniture
157–158 Martha Street, Shadwell E1
(0171) 790 3551
The owner certainly has a sense of humour here, and the outside of this railway-arch shop is strewn with left-over stage props. Inside there's a more ordinary collection of cheap chairs, tables, ovens, rugs, glassware, beds and clothes.

Cameo Galleries
108 Catford Hill, Catford SE6
(0181) 699 6668
This rag-bag of a shop's stock is mainly new – mirrors, cabinets, tables and the like – but there is a range of second-hand whites: Belling and Creda and New World free-standing ovens for £125, Hoover and Hotpoint fridge/ freezers for £120, rugs, mattresses and sofas.

The Car Boot Secondhand Shop
387 Lordship Lane, Tottenham N17
(0181) 801 5307
Furniture is the mainstay of this shop. It sells a dirt-cheap selection of three-piece living-room suites, tables, odd chairs, sideboards, mattresses and wardrobes, dating back to the Fifties or Sixties. You'll probably find the odd Formica-top Fifties kitchen table or repro mahogany veneer occasional tables. A veneer wardrobe was £40, a sideboard £15, a chest of drawers £15 and a mattress £25.

Chiswick Sale Rooms
81 Chiswick High Road, Chiswick W4
(0181) 994 01811
This mellow stripped wood shop looks frighteningly expensive, but the prices are surprisingly reasonable for the high quality involved, and the furniture is in perfect condition. Their antiques and decorative items included a rocking horse for £400, carved Victorian chairs from £60, a beechwood Victorian wardrobe for £150, and an inlaid marquetry dressing table with marble top for £160. Open daily.

D. & A. Furniture
53 Lee High Road, Lee SE13
(0181) 297 9668
Outside on the pavement are things like a Thorn gas cooker at £139, a heavy Fifties dining table at £50 and a Thirties barley twist sideboard for £130. Inside, there's a heavy emphasis on office furniture, with items like swivel chairs for £20, metal filing cabinets for £20, a roll-front wooden storage cabinet for £70, and a range of new furniture.

Dalton Antiques
2 Church Street, Lower Edmonton N9
(0181) 803 0993
Right next to Lower Edmonton British Rail station, Dalton Antiques is foremost a restorers, who sends its finished products on to other antique shops. There are some very nice pieces here that you can put in an offer on – like a huge unrestored Victorian mahogany chest of drawers for £300, or £450 restored, along with some unusual chairs, cabinets and sideboards.

G. & D. Davis Antiques
135 Bowes Road, Palmers Green N13
(0181) 889 4951
This pristine antiques shop carries a

good selection of quality pieces, mostly Victorian, such as a waist-high round table for £225, a set of five square-backed chairs, for £100, two unusual carved Victorian chairs at £45 each, or a Thirties mirror for £40.

Ed's Trading

763 Wandsworth Road, South Lambeth SW8 (0171) 498 2272

A little antiques shop that deals mainly in old pine doors from £40, some with stained glass. Other typical items include cast iron radiators for £50, a Victorian wooden cutlery tray for £65, and a carved oak overmantel for £250.

Fine Things

479 Woolwich Road, Charlton SE7 (0181) 853 4429

This cheap shop has a large range of wardrobes, dressing tables and chests of drawers, sanded down and repaired. Thirties and Fifties wardrobes start at £30, although large ones average £65, chests of drawers start at £50, sideboards at £45. A few children's bikes outside go for around £30, dining charis for £5. Free delivery within 2–3 miles.

Franklins (Camberwell Antique Market)

159–161 Camberwell Road, Camberwell SE5 (0171) 703 6429

Franklins is a Camberwell landmark, with large, rambling, tatty showrooms and a host of antiques you don't usually see in antiques shops – huge carved, brass or inlaid bedheads, massive gilt mirrors, dozens of wardrobes and odds and ends like a crystal decanter and glasses for £30, decanter stops and large dressers and sideboards: it's a real Aladdin's Cave. Bedends start at £340, Victorian dressers at £425, overmantel mirrors at £400 and antique framed prints at £20. A set of four well-restored Victorian balloon-back dining chairs was £245. There's a good café doing moderately priced snacks and full roasts on Sunday, spilling out into a rose-trailed garden, where there's garden furniture on offer.

Furniture Market

254 Acton Lane, Chiswick W4 (0181) 994 8644

This old Victorian warehouse now has a huge range of very cheap house clearance ware, ranging from furniture and crockery to officeware and the odd fireplace surround. There are shelves and shelves of glasses, china, crockery starting from 20p, dozens of books and even a shelf of dozens of cameras; and furniture of varying age and quality – such as a huge Eighties glass and teak wall unit for £135, a Thirties carved sideboard for £60, as well as dozens of wardrobes from £45, chests of drawers from £35, dining tables from £40, as well as wooden boxes, clocks, upright pianos, leather suitcases, TVs, computers or a juke box. They also have storage facilities and rent out to the film and TV industries. Open seven days a week.

The Furniture Market

7 Jerdan Place, Fulham SW6 (0171) 881 9356

One of the last few ordinary shops in this trendy enclave in Fulham, the Furniture Market has some surprisingly reasonable furniture, including, when I was there, a pair of beautiful sofas for just £400. Other items included a dining table for £60, a Seventies display cabinet at £65, mattresses starting from £15 and dining chairs at £20 each.

Furniture Mart

97 Kennington Lane, Kennington SE11 (0171) 735 5037

This crowded little shop sells mostly Sixties, Seventies and repro furniture, along with golf clubs, hoop-back chairs, ski boots and a lot of general old tat. You can wade through, though, and find the odd nice piece at a cheap price.

Furniture Mart
49 Grove Vale, East Dulwich SE22
(0181) 299 0868
A cheap junk shop with house clearance pieces – no prices are shown, so make an offer and haggle over the Forties wardrobes, dining chairs, Fifties sofas, Sixties chests of drawers, and wooden stools, Seventies chrome and black chairs. There are regular deliveries during the week, so the stock changes all the time.

Grove Green Antiques
108 Grove Green Road, Leyton E11
(0181) 558 7885
On the corner of Francis Road, this wacky antiques shop is worth travelling to, if only for the atmosphere – its setting is an old house, and you weave your way from room to room crammed full of furniture. Some walls are painted with murals, some washed with deep striking colours, and there never seems anyone about to serve you. The well-finished and restored furniture features some interesting large pieces, with much pine, and many old carved mahogany Victorian items: there was a cabinet for £265, a wardrobe for £135, a chest of drawers for £250, and a pine corner cupboard for £275. There's an extra room in the back with dozens of piled-up pieces.

Grove Vale Furniture Store
52 Grove Vale, East Dulwich SE22
(0181) 299 2515

Mainly Thirties to Fifties antiques in good condition in this small, local house removals shop. There was an old screen covered in damask, leather-covered dining chairs, easy chairs, lamps, brass chandeliers, display cabinets, clocks, marble bookcases and sofas.

Dighton Hayward Antiques
356 Upper Richmond Road, Mortlake SW14 (0181) 878 0442
A small antique shop with not much stock, Dighton Hayward does a good line in painted and antiqued secondhand furniture that is a good bargain compared with the equivalent M & S or John Lewis aged pieces. Green painted Victorian dressers started at £300, a pine marble top Victorian sidetable was £250, and a massive and beautifully restored oak tallboy was £995.

Helius Antiques
487–493 Upper Richmond Road, Mortlake SW14 (0181) 876 5721
This excellent-value shop covers four premises and features top-quality antique furniture in no-frills surrounds. You'll typically find pieces like a large mahogany dining table for £200, a mahogany veneer inlaid desk for £150, a large carved wingback chair for £95 or a set of beautifully carved Victorian balloonback chairs for £200. One of the shops features pieces in worse condition, like a rusted cast-iron fire surround, battered Fifties living-room armchairs, old trunks and books at suitably knocked-down prices.

Henry's Secondhand Shop
166a Merton Road, Merton SW19
(0181) 543 3690
Henry stocks everything you'll need in your home, like fridges, fridge freezers, velour lounge suites, TVs or microwaves, all modern and in reasonable condition. In fact, you

probably won't find anything here more than fifteen years old.

Hibs Furnishers
329 Green Lanes, Finsbury Park N4 (0181) 880 2098
This old-fashioned junk shop, right next to Finsbury park, has a range of washing machines, fridges, mattresses and furniture such as tables, cabinets, lounge suites and dining chairs.

D.W. Holmes Antique Beds
112–114 Blackheath Road, Greenwich SE10 (0181) 469 0074
These two shops knocked together specialize in antique beds from the 1850s to the turn of the century, and fireplaces from the Regency period to the early twentieth century. Beautifully restored cast-iron, brass and intricately carved wooden beds of mostly English and Irish manufacture start at £275 for a cast iron single and £535 for a double. The pieces are well restored and presented; the shop also does a part exchange scheme for old beds. The fireplaces start at around £550 for a marble Victorian surround, cast-iron inserts start at £195 and there is a fitting service provided.

Homan and Co
76 Cricklewood Broadway, Cricklewood NW2 (0181) 450 9844
Mainly modern furniture like three-piece suites and laminated tables and cabinets here. Dirt cheap and not the best of quality, but you could furnish a house for next to nothing using these people as your inspiration. I saw a fridge for £20, a Thirties oak table for £25, a red velour sofa for £125 and wardrobes at £15. At the back of the shop is a small passageway filled with mattresses and bases, starting at £20 for a single mattress and £15 for a single base. The one surprise there was a magnificent late Victorian sideboard with scrolls, pediments and carving for a mere £75.

Just Sofas
216 New King's Road, Fulham SW6 (0171) 731 5606
Close to Putney Bridge tube station, this specialist shop stocks an interesting range of good, traditional-style armchairs, sofas and divans, at excellent prices compared with new ones and including some very attractive pieces. There was a wing-back damask covered armchair from £90, a two-seater red damask sofa for £375, two carved Victorian dining chairs in red velvet for £80 each, a Sixties armchair for £20, a wing-back armchair for £85 and an IKEA-style three-seater sofa for £170. For those with sofas to sell, there's immediate collection, and there's also a covering and reupholstery service available.

K Furniture
83 Greenford Avenue, Hanwell W7 (081 567 76640
A shop with an interesting mix of Eighties junk and the odd Forties or Fifties piece of furniture, silver cutlery, lots of crystal and china ornaments, the odd Victorian wardrobe, Edwardian chairs and repro cabinets. Make an offer and haggle.

Kenways Furniture
111, 119 and 121 The Broadway, Hanwell W7 (0181) 843 9975
The Kenway empire stretches over three shops in the main road in Hanwell, and they're filled with good value furniture, some whites, and a few household knick-knacks. A set of four Thirties chairs was £39, an oak chest of drawers £75, a velvet armchair £15, a Fagor oven £119, a dining table and six chairs £90, a New World gas oven £150, wooden chairs £10 each and a trunk £35.

KNB Furniture
97 Greenford Avenue, Hanwell W7
(0181) 566 4670
This removals shop has a range of household goods from kettles, lamps, whites and wall units, all relatively new, to the odd Victorian or Thirties piece. A small Lec fridge was £45, a Prestige electric organ £135, an Electrolux vacuum cleaner £25 and an Eighties large wall unit £160.

William McGovern and Co Ltd
221 Belsize Road, Kilburn NW6 (0171) 624 4491
After thirty years in the business, the owners of this shop next to a disused railway station just off the Kilburn High Street know their stock. They specialize in domestic furniture and appliances – beds, cookers, wardrobes, cabinets. You'll find pieces in need of attention at keen prices, like a chest of drawers for £35, dressing tables from £30 or a very old television in wooden case for £65. Free delivery.

Memories
31 Willesden Lane, Kilburn NW6 (0171) 625 5494
There aren't many memories in this second-hand modern furniture shop: in fact the stock is very new and has a high turnover. It's not high in the quality department, but the furniture here doesn't tend to be that old, and is reasonably cheap and in good condition. A laminated cabinet was £50, a laminated coffee table £18, a wardrobe £45, a microwave £85, a portable TV £26 and a bedside table £20.

H.J. Morgan
21 The Broadway, Hanwell W7 (0181) 567 1557
This furniture warehouse sells cheap new furniture on the ground floor, but upstairs also has a reasonable range of second-hand cast-offs, mostly Sixties, Seventies and Eighties models. A Sixties drinks cabinet cost £100, a Sixties chest of drawers £60, a huge Fifties walnut wardrobe £80, a Sixties dressing table £20, and a Fifties chest of drawers £35.

MW Traders
299 Munster Road, Fulham SW6 (0171) 610 2030
Just off Lillie Road, this shop has lots of pine furniture stripped, half-stripped or waiting to be stripped – chairs, old trunks, tables, chests of drawers and sideboards. Some furniture has been painted in an appropriate antique finish, some varnished, and the finished products are a joy to behold. A round stripped pine Victorian table was £280 and chest of drawers was £100.

My Old China
435b Uxbridge Road, Ealing W5 (0181) 840 5984
This house clearance place is jam-packed with removal furniture, some of it very good quality, reflecting the W5 postcode. It had a Victorian commode set and copper fire accessories.

New Cross Bargain Centre
139–143 Lewisham Way, New Cross SE14 (0181) 692 8103
This large store has for over twenty years been trading house clearance merchandise, hence the mounds of tables, chairs, cabinets, rugs, clocks and small items like cutlery, ornaments and writing sets you'll find crammed in here. The store has now branched out to include new lounge suites from £199 and single divans from £40, but the emphasis is still on the pre-used. Searching through the bargain basement downstairs is like

rifling through someone's cellar, but it has plenty of furniture from the Sixties and Seventies for next to nothing. The owners say they are 'flexible' over pricing, and a bit of haggling goes a long way – I picked up a Victorian mahogany veneer cabinet for £30, and the owner drove me and it home!

Nothing New
12 Turnham Green Terrace, Turnham Green W4 (0181) 742 7277
This rambling old shop was started up by an engineer whose ambition was to trade second-hand furniture. It's a real rag-bag of large items, but for furnishing a home basically with stuff from the Fifties, Sixties and Seventies (with a few older pieces), it can't be beaten. I saw a red velour lounge suite for £175, a single bed for £35, a Sixties bureau for £45, a sofa bed for £45, a Victorian silk screen for £80, a Lec freezer for £85, a Kelvinator fridge/freezer for £95, and a Hotpoint washing machine £175. There were some men's suits, records and books downstairs. The furniture is in good condition but needs a bit of a scrub and maybe some repairing.

Now and Then
72 Norwood High Street, Upper Norwood SE27 (0181) 766 6933
A house-clearance place with some interesting stock, like a Thirties oak bedhead and foot with mattress for £145, a Seventies sofa and two easy chairs in pristine condition for £195, an Indesit washer/drier for £110, a Creda washer for £65, a Deltaware microwave for £70, and a white laminated wardrobe for £40.

Office and Household Furniture
335 Kingston Road, Wimbledon Chase SW19 (0181) 543 6066
This is serious office furniture here, with filing cabinets, swivel chairs, hatstands and desks, with the odd lounge suite or dining table thrown in for good measure.

The Old Cinema
157 Tower Bridge Road, Bermondsey SE1 (0171) 407 5371
This huge barn of a place has an excellent range of very cheap and good quality antique furniture in an old cinema building on three floors. Victorian sofas go for a very reasonable £420, an elaborate carved Edwardian sofa for £360, sideboards from £200, a set of four mahogany dining chairs £400, mahogany dressing table for £1650, Victorian Blüthner piano £2500, or an inlaid commode with a marble top £2460. It's a bit like an antique Ikea. Open seven days a week.

The Old Cinema
160 Chiswick High Road, Chiswick W4 (0181) 995 4166
This 10,000-square-foot upmarket antiques emporium is housed in a magnificent building converted from an old cinema, with *trompe-l'oeil* murals creeping up every wall, and boasts of being London's only antique department store. The stock is of high quality, mainly big Victorian pieces with some flamboyant articles from your average stately home, and although it is not cheap, the furniture is beautifully preserved; it included a late nineteenth-century mahogany inlaid bed for £295, a walnut mid Victorian dining table for £1650, a wrought iron bench for £1650, a huge Victorian mahogany chest of drawers for £895, and a Victorian rosewood round table and four chairs for £1395. Deliveries worldwide. Open seven days a week.

The Old Furniture Store
410 St John Street, Clerkenwell EC1 (0171) 713 1378

There isn't that much stock here: tables, desks, chests of drawers and cabinets, mostly made from pine and mainly dating back fifty to seventy years. They renovate it all themselves, and do a good, thorough job.

The Old Furniture Store
312 Essex Road, Islington N1
(0171) 226 6133
Everything is covered in dust in this old shop, but there's a range of nicely restored wall cabinets, chests of drawers, dining chairs, wardrobes and trunks – mostly in dark wood, but there is some pine.

Olivers
17 Woodhouse Road, Woodside Park N12 (0181) 445 2177
Just off Tally Ho Corner, this small, tatty house-clearance shop deals in second-hand furniture perfect for setting up home for the first time. It is filled with chandeliers, wardrobes, glasses, lamps and the odd oven. There were pine chests of drawers, almost new and in perfect condition, for just £175, an older standard lamp with carved base and pedestal £65, a carved dresser at £150 and a Victorian gatefold table at £55.

Oola Boola
166 Tower Bridge Road, Bermondsey SE1 (0171) 403 0794
This large warehouse-like showroom appeals to foreigners wanting to export, as the signs outside in multifarious tongues demonstrate. The smell of wax and polish permeates here, and the usual collection of wardrobes, chairs, sideboards and so on prevail. A Victorian balloon back-chair was £95, indicating not brilliant prices.

Plaistow Discount Centre
173 Plaistow Road, Plaistow E13
(0171) 519 5837
A canopied corner shop selling furniture of surprisingly high quality – I spotted a stunning Edwardian oak folding barley-twist dining table and four carved Victorian chairs for only £145. You'll find the odd TV, fridge, 3-in-1 stereo, washing machine and lounge suite in here at equally competitive prices.

Powers Furniture
46 Cricklewood Broadway, Cricklewood NW2 (0181) 452 1058
The modern second-hand furniture that this shop stocks is piled high on the pavement on Cricklewood's main road, and there are plenty of reasonably priced items like wardrobes, chairs, tables, and even the odd piano.

Quality Bargains
127 Peckham High Street, Peckham SE15 (0171) 732 5741
This tatty high-street house clearance shop stocks mainly Sixties and Seventies goods like wardrobes (£35), bureaux (£40) and chests of drawers (£30). The furniture is strictly utilitarian, but it's a dirt-cheap way to furnish your home.

Revivals
181 Lavender Hill, Battersea SW11
(0171) 924 7644
A removals shop with plenty of unusual Fifties and Sixties stock in good condition and keenly priced. There's a profusion of Fifties furniture, with things like a standard lamp, an oak sideboard, or a vinyl and wool lounge suite. A large Fifties wardrobe goes for around £55, a dining table for £55 and a Sixties kitsch drinks bar for £145.

Second Time Around
35 Essex Road, Islington N1
(0171) 354 9398
The furniture is cheap here – you won't find any cheaper in upmarket

Issie – like a three seater green velour sofa and armchair for £85, a green glazed Victorian stove for £175, an Indesit freezer for £60, a two-seater leather sofa for £65, antique Victorian carved chairs – admittedly not in perfect condition – for £35 each, and a Sixties display cabinet for £60.

Second Time Around
110 Lewisham Way, New Cross SE14
(0181) 469 0848
Jam-packed little house clearance shop with so many second-hand mattresses that you can't see anything or move round much. The quality is variable, but there is the odd piece worth looking at. Lots of Fifties tat.

The Secondhand Furniture Shop
356 Kilburn High Road, Kilburn NW6
(0171) 625 9682
Next to the railway bridge over the high street, this second-hand shop stocks mainly modern domestic furniture, and some new pieces. It's all in good condition – in fact very good condition – and there are a few antique pieces at low prices that you'd need to renovate yourself. A white dining suite with four grey covered chairs was £100, a large white Ikea bookcase £30, a small bookcase £15, small fridge/freezers from £60, and four Victorian leather covered dining chairs £50.

The Secondhand Shop
172–174 Stoke Newington High Street, Stoke Newington N16 (0171) 249 7607
In this large showroom is a wide range of pieces of varying quality, but most of them larger items of furniture like chests of drawers, sideboards, wardrobes, cabinets, mirrors, dining suites, lounge suites and dressing tables, all ranging from Fifties clutter to some genuine Victorian pieces. Prices are all negotiable.

The Secondhand Shop
17 Walm Lane, Willesden Green NW2
(0181) 459 7583
A removal shop pushing a tacky collection of twenty-year-old furniture like sculptured living-room suites, teak and glass coffee tables, a typewriter, a Seventies 3-in-1 stereo, wall cabinets, or an Ikea-style chest of drawers. Down the alleyway at the side of the shop are dozens of whites – fridges, fridge/freezers, washing machines and ovens. There's the odd older dining chair or cabinet that could be nice when renovated, and the prices are very low.

William Slemmonds and Son
136 Upper Richmond Road, Mortlake SW14 (0181) 878 8988
The owner of this house clearance shop has an excellent eye and pieces here are of very good quality and surprisingly well priced. A stunning rectangular solid mahogany Victorian dining table – nicely restored and French polished – was just £325, an inlaid mahogany veneer wardrobe £175, a large pine trunk cost £175, a mahogany covered overmantel £275, and a large stripped pine mirror £65. They also do furniture restoration and French polishing on the premises.

S.P. Furniture
Cornwall Road, off Watney Street, Shadwell E1 (0171) 702 7152
Next to Shadwell British Rail station is this half-outdoor furniture house clearance place in an out-of-the-way location – with a bit of everything. It sells mainly Thirtes to Seventies tat, electrical appliances, doors, dog kennels, gas bottles, and some new beds. Typically, you'll find a small fridge/freezer from £35, ovens from £50, with three- to six-month guarantees. A wardrobe will start at £30

and sideboards from £35; new beds go for £70. Delivery is free within a five-mile radius. There are some surprises like a Victorian carved rosewood sideboard at £75.

Traders New and Used Furniture
31–33 Woolwich Road, Greenwich SE10 (0181) 858 4719
It's impossible to see anything in this little shop as it's jam-packed into a small space, but you can make out the outlines of living-room suites, cupboards, Sixties veneer tables, mattresses and freestanding ovens in amongst it all. Bottom-of-the-range furniture at good prices in varying conditions.

Trading Post
215–217 Rye Lane, Peckham SE15 (0171) 732 6494
You'll find Sixties and Seventies wooden furniture like chests of drawers for £30, dressing tables for £35, wardrobes for £50 and wicker chairs for £35, and the odd nice piece, like a Thirties carved sideboard for £40. Junk of good quality.

Trading Post
47 Charlton Church Lane, Charlton SE7 (0181) 853 5662
This little local shop at the heart of Charlton village trades almost anything from furniture, records and clothes to electrical appliances and videos. Records go for £2, videos for £3, new beds from £65, and a used fridge was £135.

Victoriana
90 Kingston Road, Merton SW19 (081) 540 9969
This genteel little antiques shop sells at reasonable prices, and some of the furniture is quite unusual. A Victorian velour sofa was £120, a set of four Edwardian dining chairs £85, an oak Edwardian chest of drawers £150, an oak overmantel with shelf and mirror £85, an oak bevelled mirror £20 and fire utensils £25.

H.T. Whitewood and Son
43 High Road, Lee SE12 (0181) 852 0467
Very much lower-range stuff. It had a coffee table for just £5, a desk at £20, an old-fashioned pram for £95, Victorian pine bookshelves for £59, old wooden chairs for £5 and a new calico sofa for £125.

World of Furniture
172 Harrow Road, Kensal Green NW10 (0181) 961 8762
A mixture of new and cheap second-hand furniture, like sofa beds from £145, side tables at £9, wooden tables from £20, 3-in-1 stereos from £25 and TVs from just £30.

Yesterdays
315 Upper Richmond Road West, Mortlake SW14 (0181) 876 7536
A pine specialist shop with a large stock, including pine dressers, chests of drawers, tables, chairs, trunks and desks, all stripped and restored or varnished. The prices here reflect the quality of the pieces: huge Victorian pine trunks at £220, large Victorian wardrobes at £685, a dressing table and carved mirror for £280 and an old timber dresser for £545. The basement downstairs features more pine, but there are new pieces mixed with the old.

Your Second-hand Furniture
138 Kingston Road, Merton SW19 (0181) 543 7286
This excellent furniture shop sells no-frills merchandise in good condition at bargain prices. A large coffee table with Seventies-style Egyptian mosaics on top was just £10, a wooden chair

£2, a Thirties Art Deco sideboard £65, modern wardrobes £40, a wooden fireguard £5, a nicely carved Victorian wardrobe with a long mirror £120, a black-and-white TV £25, and a side table £15.

JEWELLERY

Most jewellers don't deal in second-hand jewellery, but there are some outlets through the capital that trade specifically in – or carry a stock of – old rings, watches, necklaces and clocks, and you can often pick up a Victorian item for less than it would cost brand new. Note that jewellery prices vary according to the current trading price of gold.

Attenborough
207 High Holborn, Holborn WC1
(0171) 405 7048
A generous array of women's brooches and rings of varying ages is a feature in the window of this city jeweller. They have some very nice quality pieces: I saw a cameo brooch at £79, a lapis lazuli brooch at £149, an oval garnet brooch at £195, a stone-set brooch at £179, a 9ct gold locket brooch at £135, garnet stud earrings at £132 and amethyst drop earrings at £140.

Also at 193 Fleet Street, EC4
(0171) 405 1696

Austin Kaye and Co
425 The Strand, Covent Garden WC2
(0171) 240 1888
A jewellery and watch specialist since 1946, Austin Kaye buys, sells and part-exchanges quality second-hand watches.

J.J. Barrett and Sons
271 Caledonian Road, Holloway N7
Pawnbroker with a small selection of second-hand rings and a huge sign extolling Ronson lighters. Most of the rings are 9ct gold – men's and women's – but some have onyx, zircon or other stones. Also sells new lighters, clocks and silverware.

Carnel Watchmaker and Jewellers
107 Fortis Green Road, Muswell Hill N10
This old-fashioned jewellers' shop is big enough for one person at a time – if there are more, you will have a claustrophobic crisis. The owner, Lionel Woolf, is a talkative man whose passion for clocks and watches has lasted for over forty years. His clocks range from familiar upturned parabola Thirties Westminster chimes to bracket clocks, carved Victorian ones and more elaborate marble and gilt varieties. Victorian clocks average at about £125, a 140-year-old alabaster clock was £400. Westminster chimes go for around £75. Clocks are restored and overhauled, and generally come with a one-year guarantee.

Cash Converters
292–294 Lewisham High Street, Lewisham SE13 (0181) 690 9800
This new-fangled chain of pawnbrokers buys and sells almost anything of value, and the large stock suggests that the locals make the most of it. There are stacks of bikes, TVs, stereos, videos, rings, toys, cameras and computers in good condition and fairly new. There are no dirt-cheap bargains here, but it does offer value for money: you

might snap up a Sony remote control TV for £119, a Casio tonebank keyboard for £75, a Goodmans graphic equalizer for £69 or an electronic typewriter for £89.

City Pledge
363 St John Street, Clerkenwell EC1
(0171) 833 4554
Right on the Angel intersection, this former pub turned pawnbrokers now deals mainly in musical instruments, like guitars, brass instruments, violins, keyboards and wind instruments, as well as a small selection of watches, earrings, rings, necklaces, lighters and video equipment – jewellery starts at £25, with items like a gold Omega watch at £495 (half RRP).

Clarks Jewellers
201 Maple Road, Penge SE20 (0181) 778 5935
A jeweller's with a good range of traded-in pieces, ranging from rings and chains to watches and silver pill boxes. Typical finds might include a 9ct gold ring with elaborate opal set with small diamonds for £80, a 9ct gold ring with two emeralds at £145, quartz ring for £38.50, or a garnet ring at £25.50. There are lots of bracelets, necklaces and chains for sale, as well as some hallmarked solid silver pill boxes for around £20. Everything that's second-hand is marked.

J. Courtney
31 Pembridge Road, Notting Hill W11
Mr Courtney specializes in silver, and stocks cutlery, jewellery, tea and coffee services, trinkets and the like. A silver sauce ladle cost £9, a serving spoon £8, a silver-plated King's pattern 62-piece cutlery set £320, a silver-plated four-piece tea and coffee set £55, a tray £64, a silver-plated cream jug, sugar bowl and tray £11, a huge silver-plated soup ladle £35 and a silver-plated champagne cooler £95.

Feinmesser Jewellers
34a Cranbourn Street, Covent Garden WC2 (0171) 836 8283
Just by Leicester Square tube station, this small jeweller's shop displays a range of its second-hand rings, brooches and cufflinks in the window. Typical pieces include a ring with a huge amethyst surrounded by small pearls for £100 or a Victorian brooch for £85.

Hilda Freeman Antiques
24 The Green, Winchmore Hill N21
(0181) 886 0925
A theatrical sort of shop on Winchmore Hill's provincial green, with a range of fine clocks, silverware, watches, china and crystal. Watches start from around £20 and date back as far as the 1930s. There are fancy rings from £30, silver ladles and figurines from £25.

H.W. Godfrey and Son
331 Walworth Road, Walworth SE17
A jeweller's shop on the busy main road, selling a large range of second-hand goodies like 9ct gold men's rings from £30, with opal, amethyst, engraved and plain examples. There are women's rings with settings like diamonds and emerald for £145, diamond and ruby for £145, 18ct gold with two diamonds for £195, and bracelets, earrings, pendants, new watches and chains – also picture frames.

Gold Mine Bullion Buyers
150 Old Kent Road, New Cross SE14
(0171) 732 1777
An all-rounder, dealing in not only gold and jewellery, but also mobile phones, clocks, paintings, chairs, bookcases, mirrors, china, toys, tea-

pots, tapestries, snuff boxes, instruments, teddy bears and old dolls.

Goldmine Discount Jewellers
57 Mile End Road, Bow E3
(0171) 791 1581
A little local jeweller, selling a small but interesting array of antique jewellery, as well as doing watch repairs.

Thomas Kettle's
53a Neal Street, Covent Garden WC2
(0171) 379 3579
This Covent Garden institution was specializing in vintage and classic wristwatches and designing its own jewellery long before this area became trendy. It stocks the best in pre-used watches – Longines, Omega, Rolex and classic American makes – from the 1920s onwards. A Rolex Oyster Imperial (1935) goes for £925, an Omega 14ct gold (1945) for £925 and a Ralco travel watch (1940) for £400. Prices average around £400 but can go up to £10,000 for rare items. Other merchandise includes new cufflinks, hand-painted ties (£40), silver jewellery, wedding rings and contemporary paintings.

J.A. Lake
33 Camden High Street, Camden Town NW1 (0171) 387 3871
A great selection of men's signet rings, ladies' fancy and plain gold bands, ladies' and children's signets, silver settings with semi-precious stones, stud earrings, chains, charms, necklaces, Victorian engagement rings, Victorian and Edwardian jewellery, lockets, fob watches, crosses, dress rings with gemstones, watches, clocks and pendants.

A. & H. Page
66 Gloucester Road, South Kensington SW7 (0171) 584 7349
A ten-minute walk from Gloucester Road tube station, this jeweller has rings, earrings, picture frames and watches of good quality. A few gold men's rings go for around £100, women's rings in 9ct gold for £75, earrings from £70; a Cartier watch was £1250 (new price £1995).

Reem Jewellers
10 Star Street, Paddington W2
(0171) 723 9100
A small jeweller's shop dealing in gold, silver, diamonds, clocks and watches of all ages.

South Kensington Jewellers
11 Bute Street, South Kensington SW7
(0171) 589 8856
This fine antique jewellery shop, just round the corner from South Kensington tube, has a shimmering collection of stunning jewellery, watches, clocks, picture frames and the like. The watches, with brand names like Rolex and Cartier, start at £295 and go up to thousands for a fine diamond studded timepiece. Likewise the rings – a plain 9ct gold signet ring can go for £70, but there are sapphires, emeralds and diamonds in the thousands. Cameos start at £150, cufflinks from £70.

Steinberg and Tolkien
193 King's Road, Chelsea SW3
(0171) 376 3660
This fascinating shop stocks London's biggest selection of women's US designer costume jewellery dating from the Twenties to the Fifties, concentrating on design and quality of craftsmanship. Display cases dazzle with high-quality Chanel, Dior, Schiaperelli and Tifari earrings, necklaces, brooches and rings. Not the shop for someone who wants a necklace to match their eyes – beware, the owner bites! Prices are anything from

£5 to £7000 for a rare piece, reflecting the high quality of merchandise. The shop also stocks a small range of men's designer garments, like Chanel 1935 men's vintage designer ties from £12 and cufflinks for £15–30.

G.W. and A.E. Thomson

36 Chalk Farm Road, Chalk Farm NW1
(0171) 485 2668

This chain of shops was established back in 1837 and has been pawnbroking ever since, specializing in pledges (when people need a loan and pawn their valuables, and never come back). There is an interesting array of diamond rings, ornate fobs, gold chains and other jewellery in the window. Inside are cameras, musical instruments, binoculars, silverware, a few clocks, the occasional Rolex or Cartier, and things like silver letter clasps. Prices fluctuate with the gold index, but you could expect to pay around £25 for gold necklaces or £30 for rings. Secondhand cameras are around 25 percent less than you'd pay new.

Also at 63 Praed Street, Paddington W2; 158 Portobello Road W11.

MUSICAL INSTRUMENTS

Shops selling musical instruments are mainly based in Soho, around Denmark Street and along Charing Cross Road, but if you comb some of the suburbs you'll find similar merchandise at more competitive prices.

Andy's Guitar Centre and Workshop
27 Denmark Street, Covent Garden WC2 (0171) 916 5080
With its enviable selection of guitars acoustic and electric, this is the most renowned guitar shop in London. Andy Preston began repairing guitars in his basement in the late 1970s, and the business has spread into two floors of cluttered guitars standing up like tombstones, with a few second-hand amps usually sitting in the passageway outside. There are electric guitars like a Tobas, a Wilkes, a Sixties Silvertone, a Gibson Firebird, a Yamaha six-string bass, a Sixties Ampeg, a 1956 Fender Esquire, a left-hand Hohner headless, a Sixties Coral Star, a Sixties Fender Jaguar and a Sixties Vox Phantom. The acoustics section is upstairs, featuring a more limited – and mostly new – selection of Condé Hermanos, Gibson, Martin, Regal and Sigma, with a small group of mandolins. Most come with a twelve-month guarantee, and there's a unique find a guitar service.

Boogie
25 Denmark Street, Covent Garden WC2 (0171) 240 3309
Mainly electric guitars and second-hand amplifiers. Cash is paid for used guitars; there is also a part-exchange scheme.

Hank's Guitar Shop
24 Denmark Street, Covent Garden WC2 (0171) 379 1139
Hank claims to be England's largest stockist of Francis, Guild, Gibson, Martin Larrivée, Lowden, Washburn and Yamaha models, and to have the best prices in town. There's a reasonable selection of new and second-hand, and cash is paid for guitars. The acoustic department is downstairs in the basement.

H.P. Hayward and Sons
559 Wandsworth Road, South Lambeth SW8 (0171) 622 2426
In a little alleyway off the main road are the piano workshops of this small showroom which stocks mainly British and German pianos like Bluthners and Obermeiers, all retuned, their cases restored and restrung if necessary. Small uprights and grands can be anything up to 100 years old. Open seven days a week.

Kirkdale Pianos
251 Dartmouth Road, Sydenham SE26 (0181) 699 1928
A cheap upright specialist. All pianos are reconditioned and come with guarantees.

London Rock Shop
26 Chalk Farm Road, Camden Town NW1 (0171) 267 5381

An acoustic guitar and drum kit shop on Chalk Farm Road. Goods included old Marshall amps from £200 and a Peavey Solo 10/15 battery mains combo for £95. Closed on Mondays.

Lowes

102 Greenwich South Street, Greenwich SE10 (0181) 691 6944

A sundry collection of woodwind instruments, including saxophones, flutes, clarinets, flutes and oboes.

Macari's Musical Instruments

92–94 Charing Cross Road, Covent Garden WC2 (0171) 836 2856

A well-established music shop, with a good selection of instruments, especially vintage guitars, along with accordions, oboes, trumpets, saxes and vintage combos. You'll typically find gear like a 1964 Epiphone Casina at £795, a 1967 Gibson ES 345 for £1299, a Washburn KC40V at £199, a Hohner Acoustic for £75, a Lap harp for £199, a Höfner Ambassador around 1967 for £345, a Burns of London Scorpion Bass 1976 for £695, a 1965 Guild T100D jazz and rock 'n' roll guitar for £645, a Yamaha clarinet for £395, a Gemindhardt silver plated flute for £199, a 1920 British mando-banjo for £210 or an antique Neapolitan mandolin at £165.

Music Exchange

56 Notting Hill Gate, Notting Hill W11 (0171) 229 4808

A part of the massive Exchange network in Notting Hill, this branch sells musical instruments, books and comics. Musical stock included microphones from £90, a tenor sax for £450, castanettes for £2, a flute for £250, and amplifiers for £180. Upstairs, there is general paperback fiction from £1 and comics starting from 50p, including *The Hulk*, *Spiderman* and *Flash Gordon*, and another room filled with 50p bargain books and 10p comics. Open seven days a week.

Muswell Hill Pianos

300 Muswell Hill Broadway, Muswell Hill N10 (0181) 883 6020

Right on the Muswell Hill roundabout, this shop on two floors sells a wide range of new and used pianos, including good quality reconditioned German and English makes of uprights and grands, many in traditional cases, with wood and finishes not available today, like a Wilson Peck straight-strung overdamped black upright for £895, a Blüthner straight-strung underdamped rosewood case for £3250. It also sells some refurbished piano stools.

The Piano Workshop

30a Highgate Road, Kentish Town NW5 (0171) 267 7671

Tucked away in a mews opposite the Forum, this building has been associated with pianos for 150 years, when it started off as a piano manufacturer. It now offers a selection of upright or grand pianos, all restored – sometimes rehammered, restrung, keys replaced, casing overhauled – on two floors of showrooms, in a peaceful, if slightly overheated setting. A good basic, straight-strung piano starts at £750, a decent overstrung upright at £1000 (English) and £1600 (German); grand pianos start at £2500 for an English make and £3000 for a German one. They stock makes like Blüthner, Fuchs and Mohr, Hoffman, Knight, Rippen, Schimmel, Weber and Young Chang. Delivery is promised within four days, and part-exchange and short-term hire is possible.

Piano World

60 Chalk Farm Road, Camden Town NW1 (0171) 485 1555

New and second-hand pianos, like

Bechstein, Blüthner, Calles, Knight and Yamahas for sale or hire. Open seven days a week.

Polymart
109 Clapham High Street, Clapham SW4 (0171) 622 5015
This shop, which has been around since 1955, stocks a range of electric guitars in its tiny premises. It also stocks a small selection of cassettes at £3, CDs at £5, and oddments like a Hanimex camera for £14.50 and a gig box for £18.

Pro-Brass Ltd
2 Highgate Road, Kentish Town NW5 (0171) 482 1055
A brass and woodwind shop on the junction at Kentish Town. Downstairs are the brass and woodwind instruments, all tested and guaranteed, with a range of saxes, electric guitars and French horns. Upstairs on the ground floor are new drum kits and electric guitars. There's a music room to try out your purchase.

Rock Around the Clock
11 Park Road, Crouch End N8 (0181) 292 8484
New guitars comprise most of the stock here, but the shop carries a dozen or so used models which tend to be cheaper than in the West End. You'll typically find a Fender-Stratocaster 1962 for £1275, a Gibson 355 from the Seventies for £899, a Fifites Hofner for £399, a 79 anniversary Fender-Stratocaster for £550, a Washburn for £899 or a 1957 Fender-Stratocaster for £3500. In the amp department, you'll find a Seventies Fender-Stratocaster twin reverb for £399, or a Marshall artist 50-watt head £275. There's a room at the back of the shop where people can try out instruments without fear of being listened to.

Len Stites
272 Lewisham High Street, Lewisham, SE13
Mostly stocking new instrments and sheet music, this large shop also carries some second-hand reconditioned models: it had, for example, a Sapphire flute for £175, a clarinet for £155, a Yamaha electrone for £295 and French horn for £299. It also stocks new drum kits, guitars (electric and classical), brass instruments, keyboards and session players.

Tin Pan Alley
23 Denmark Street, Covent Garden WC2 (0171) 240 3483
Tin Pan Alley has a huge selection of discounted equipment, including microphones, mixers, speakers, electric and acoustic guitars, with weekly specials on particular brands. In the cellar are basses and drums.

Tune Inn
124–126 St Mildred's Road, Lee SE13 (0181) 698 4446
A range of keyboards, guitars, TVs, videos, lights and stereos.

West End Music Exchange
106 Charing Cross Road, Covent Garden WC2 (0171) 836 8198
There are plenty of guitars, drum machines, amps, speakers and professional recording equipment here. You might find a 1975 Fender Ash strat for around £399, a five-string bass at £799, an Alesis drum machine for £159, a Bel digital processor for £299, a Yamaha digital rhythm programmer for £159 or a digital rhythm recorder for £99, as well as acoustic guitars from £199.

PHOTOGRAPHIC

Second-hand camera equipment is not generally something for the novice – there's a staggering range of top-quality gear at horrific prices, broken down into bodies and a bewildering array of lenses, tripods and filters – and many of the camera shops listed below are places for semi-professionals. But most will sell a few instamatic models that have been reconditioned and tested, more suitable for the amateur.

Camden Camera Centre
45c Parkway, Camden Town NW1
(0171) 485 7247
This small shop had a range of second-hand cameras and lenses in the window ranging from an Olympus OM10 50mm 1.8 for £89.99 to an old Lubitel 166U for £29.99. Lenses start at £29.99.

Chiswick Camera Centre
5 Chiswick Terrace, Acton Lane, Chiswick W4 (0181) 995 9114
This is a specialist dealer in new and second-hand lenses, binoculars, projectors and cameras, and had models like a Ricoh Mirai for £189, a Kodak Instamatic 500 for £99, a Konica Auto Reflex A for £99, a Nikon EM Vivitar for £189 and a Fuji DL-30 Autofocus for £42.

Fox Talbot
443 Strand, Covent Garden WC2
(0171) 379 6522
This well-respected chain of camera shops has a very good range of top quality camera equipment, along with a few cheaper no-fuss cameras for the photographically challenged. A wide selection of good-quality lenses features models from a Canon 35-70 'A' AF f3.5–4.4 for £70 up to a Nikon 180mm f2.8 ED AIS for £550. There are plenty of old Leica bodies, like an R-4 for £440, an R-5 + SO/F21 for £1195 and a Nikon 123 body at £499. More modest are the Minolta bodies that go from £95. Quentin batteries start at £99, and there's a range of cheaper cameras like Monoltas from £40 and a Canon Epoca that was £139.

Also at 67 New Oxford Street, Holborn W1.

Ivor Howell Cameras
397 Lewisham High Street, Lewisham SE13 (0181) 690 2780
A very good range of second-hand cameras at reasonable prices, with names like Minolta, Pentax, Ricoh, Tauron and Yashica. An Olympus FT-L50 was £119, an OM 707 Body £99.95, a Ricoh XRX Body 35-70 zoom £199.95, and a Practica BX 20 50mm £99.95. Also sells bellows, editors, filters, photosnipers, flashes and lenses.

Jessop Classic Photographica
67 Great Russell Street, Bloomsbury WC1 (0171) 831 3640
Opposite the British Museum, but entered via Pied Bull Yard, a hidden square off Bury Place, this is Europe's leading vintage camera equipment store. There is plenty of material here for nostalgia freaks, with original

Kodak Box Brownies, Nikon bodies, Canons, Purma, Alpa Reflex and Minox, along with a range of optical toys, reference books and things like magic lanterns.

Kingsley Photographic
93 Tottenham Court Road, Bloomsbury W1 (0171) 387 6500
This small shop sells second-hand Minoltas, Nikons, Pentaxes and the like, with a good range of high-quality gear. There were Minolta bodies like a 5000i for £225 and a 3000i for £185, and Pentax bodies like an SPF at £165 and a P30 at £120; Olympus lenses start at around £125 for a 28mm up to £395 for a 24mm. Video cameras featured a Canon Autozoom 512 for £135 and an Agfa movie zoom for £235.

R.G. Lewis
217 High Holborn, Holborn WC1
(0171) 242 2916
A used Leica camera specialist, with a good general range of quality camera equipment, like an Olympus OM-10 for £119, a Contax T2 for £599, a Bencini Koroll for £26, an Agfa Selecta for £35, and a Kiev 35mm lens for £70.

London Camera Exchange
112 Strand, Covent Garden WC2
(0171) 379 0200
A very professional outfit with helpful assistants and a good range of quality lenses, cameras and bodies. Lenses include everything from a Nikon Vivitar AF from £69 up to a Nikkor 100–300mm f5–6 at £399 and through to a Nikkor 400mm at £1499. You might find Leica bodies like an R-4 at £349 and an M4-P at £799, a Nikkon FTN at £99 or a Nikkormat FTN at £150. Cameras included models like a Pentax SP 500 for £69, a Minolta SRT 303b for £149 and a Chinon CP.7 at £129. There are polaroid instant cameras for £69, binoculars at £29 upwards, as well as new cameras, flashes and lenses.

Photo Optix
73 Praed Street, Paddington W2
(0171) 402 4808
A range of cameras, lenses and accessories, tripods, opera glasses, winders, photoframes and albums. You'll typically find models like a Minolta 24 Rapid for £19.99, a Pentax ME Super Body for £79.99, a Canon Sure Shot for £49.99, a Yashica FX-3 Super for £79.99, a Nikon F2s Body for £419.99, and a Polaroid Vision for £69.99.

Also at 234 Baker Street, Euston NW1
(0171) 487 4378;
93 Edgware Road, Paddington W2
(0171) 723 2891;
187 King's Road, Chelsea SW3
(0171) 352 5756;
8 Oak Road, Ealing W5
(0181) 840 7028.

Rare Camera Co
18 Bury Place, Bloomsbury WC1
(0171) 405 8858
An interesting shop on Pied Bull Yard, off Bury Place, stocking some fascinating old cameras. There were Retinettes from £35, Minicords at £294, tiny Coonet Midgets at £90, boxy Voigtlanders at £29, old Rollei Rolleiflexes from £70 and AGI Agiflex IIIs for £145.

Vintage Cameras Ltd
256 Kirkdale, Sydenham SE26
(0181) 778 5841
This is one of south London's best second-hand camera shops, with a wide range of equipment and some really interesting early models going back 130 years. Old Kodak Brownies start at £19, an Agfa Clack was £29, a

1910 Benetfink £89. Early cine-cameras and movie cameras stand side by side with light meters and lenses. Typical finds in the more modern category include a Canon A-1 for £229, an Olympus OM-10 for £129, a Halina Pix 35mm for £6.50, or a Canon Canonet 29 for £49.

York Cameras

1 Victoria Colonnade, Southampton Row, Bloomsbury WC1 (0171) 242 7182

York Cameras has a large display of lenses and cameras. Prices started with an Olympus OM10 at £109.95, peaking with a Canon EOS 1 at £999.95.

RECORDS, CASSETTES, COMPACT DISCS and VIDEOS

See also Charity Shops *and* Junk Shops

Ever since CDs weaseled their way into the sounds arena, records have been gradually swept under the carpet – resulting in more flooding of the second-hand market as people dump their turntables and invest in digital display hi-tech. Now that LPs are no longer being produced, record collecting is a strictly retro affair, and if you missed out the first time around, now is the time to pick up second-hand David Bowie or Thompson Twins albums, as well as more specialist jazz or blues original issues. Tapes, CDs and videos go out of fashion and back in again, so there's always a big supply out there.

OTHER MUSIC AND VIDEO OUTLETS

Music and video libraries are always selling off old stock, at prices from a couple of pounds, and although the goods have been heavily used before, there is still life left in them. **Video shops** too are always selling off used stock, so keep your eye on your local *Ritz* or *Blockbuster* and pick up some big budget blockbusters from a few years ago for only £3 or £4.

James Asman Records
23a New Row, Covent Garden WC2
This very small shop just off St Martin's Lane stocks second-hand – and a smaller range of new – records, CDs and (a few) cassettes, devoted to vintage jazz, Louisiana jazz, shows/ stage, easy listening and big band sounds for around £3, and going up to £6 for rarer recordings. There was a boxed set of five LPs of Sidney Bechet in the window for £15.95. Second-hand CDs go for £6–8.

Bud's Country Music Store
184 High Street, Penge SE20
(0181) 676 8801
London's country and western fans should feel right at home in this little ol' bitty shop that's full to the gunwales with mainly new but also some second-hand country greats like Jann Browne, Eddie Cochran, Billy Dean, Patsy Kline, Brenda Lee, the Oakridge Boys and plenty more. There are racks and racks of LPs, cassettes and CDs, with some videos and books for the hard-core enthusiast. LPs and tapes range from £3.50 to £15, and CDs from £5 to £15.

Collections
70 Lee High Road, Lewisham SE13
(0181) 463 9388
This funky little shop displays Cilla Black, Bing Crosby and Gracie Fields records in the window, but inside stocks everything from R & B, punk and hip hop to golden oldies. Records are categorized up to a point, but there are unsorted boxes to wade through patiently where the Sex Pistols rub shoulders with Shirley Bassey, making this a great place to browse, but hopeless if you're a person with a mission. Tapes line the walls in much the same idiosyncratic filing system. There are collectors' copies of *Melody Maker* and books on singing stars, as well as general paperbacks from 50p. Pay the owner, who stands by the door behind a turntable keeping the music pumping. Wonderful paper bags with Greta Garbo's face on them for sale.

Collectors Records
303 Munster Road, Fulham SW6
Close to the junction with Lillie Road, this small shop doesn't have a staggering selection, but makes a pleasant enough place to browse for your favourite soul, Seventies and Eighties pop/rock, jazz or heavy metal. LPs average £5–6, singles £1.50, and a rare deletion up to £40.

Dress Circle
57–59 Monmouth Street, Covent Garden WC2 (0171) 240 2227
The basement of this excellent specialist stage 'showbiz' shop is devoted to records of mainly out-of-print vinyl recordings that haven't yet been – or won't ever be – transferred to CD. The rarity of the disc determines the price, so albums of your favourite Broadway or West End spectacles start at £1.99 and can hit the roof at £65 for a rare 'Jeeves' edition. Upstairs are new CDs of the great stage performers – everything from Garland, Piaf, Sinatra and Streisand to Italian versions of *La Cage aux Folles* or a Japanese *Miss Saigon*, heaven forbid. Collections of new posters, videos, libretti, cards, theatre books, postcards of singers and movie stars and scores are strewn everywhere. It's obviously a labour of love for its staff who sing along with the non-stop show tapes playing.

58 Dean Street
58 Dean Street, Soho W1 (0171) 437 4500
Billing itself as a specialist in nostalgia, film and shows, this jam-packed record shop is the place to go for a good selection of your favourite golden oldies from the screen – Charles Aznavour, Eve Boswell, Bing Crosby, Judy Garland, Shirley Temple or Sarah Vaughan – as well as a wide range of soundtracks from films past and present. LPs start at about £3.95, and a special sale rack flogs off a selected number from £2. Stock is divided into male vocal, female vocal, soundtracks and foreign soundtracks.

Honest Jon's Records
278 Portobello Road, Notting Hill W10
(0181) 969 9822
Honest Jon's particular fancy is a range of records: hip hop, soul, funk and jazz – soul or fusion – reggae, house and garage all selling at around £4 upwards, including names like Van Morrison, Aretha Franklin and Marvin Gaye. He also has an especially good collection of deleted jazz on vinyl as well as imports from the States. Open seven days a week.

Mole Jazz
311 Gray's Inn Road, Holborn WC1
(0171) 278 8623
A well-established trendy jazz shop revered by afficionados and stock-

ing the largest selection of jazz-related records, tapes and CDs in the UK.

Harold Moore's Records
2 Great Marlborough Street, Soho W1
(0171) 437 1370
This is the shop to go to for second-hand classical records: in the basement are hundreds of rare, deleted and just plain pre-used LPs varying in price according to rarity. The recordings are organized alphabetically into composers, with separate sections for opera, operetta, a few stage and screen records, collectors' editions and boxed sets. You might pick up a Pavarotti LP from the special clearance box for £2.50, or pay £50 for a rare deleted recording of Bruckner's Ninth. Outside there are benches clearing stock from £2.50, with a range of jazz, classical and nostalgia. On the ground floor are new CDs arranged in much the same way. Records and tapes are from £2.50; CDs £3.50 and £4.50.

Music and Video Exchange
34, 38–40, 56, 64 and 65 Notting Hill Gate, Notting Hill W11 (0171) 221 1444
14, 20 and 30 Pembridge Rd, Notting Hill W11
Owner Brian Abrams opened his first shop in 1968 to buy and sell anything second-hand, and it germinated into probably the best second-hand record chain in London, offering a comprehensive range of records, tapes, CDs and videos, with musical instruments, books, clothes and electronic equipment, scattered throughout nine shops in Notting Hill. Open seven days a week.

No. 34 offers a range of second-hand cameras and lenses, from a £20 Hanimex up to Canons and Leicas.

No. 38 is the main outlet for records, tapes, CDs and videos, with soul and dance in the basement, pop on the ground floor, and easy listening, Beatles and jazz upstairs, including rarities and deletions. There's a DJ tucked away in a little room keeping the place swinging. The records here are pricier than in the other shops, but they are gradually knocked down depending on how long they sit on the shelves. LPs are from £3, books downstairs for 10p.

No. 40 Records here are unsorted and dirt cheap, but that can be infuriating for those who don't like leafing through dozens of artists they've never heard of. 7-inch singles go for 10p, 12-inch singles for 20p, LPs from £1. The blank audio tapes are the cheapest to be found at £1 for a five-pack of 30-minute tapes and up to £2.50 for five 90-minute tapes.

No. 56 is the music exchange, stocking a small range of instruments, books and comics upstairs and an excellent range of classical records and tapes on the top floor, with piped concertos coming through speakers. There are records for 50p in a corner, but most start at £2, with boxed sets from £10.

No. 64 is the Hi-Fi Exchange, with TVs, videos and music equipment.

No. 65 on the opposite side of the road is the Computer Exchange, with computer games and hardware.

Around the corner in Pembridge Road is the Sports Exchange at no. 14, and another Music and Video Exchange at no. 20, with Retro, the second-hand clothes shop at no. 30.

Out on the Floor
10 Inverness Street, Camden Town NW1
This relaxed shop just off the High

Street has records from £5, CDs from £6.50, and a bin of both knocked down to £5. There is a small collection of tapes, and many rare records, female vocal, instrumental, rock 'n' roll, jazz, R & B and Seventies rock. Down a dizzily poky staircase are new CDs, tapes and film/pop posters from £3.50.

Ray's Jazz Shop
180 Charing Cross Road, Covent Garden WC2 (0171) 240 3969
A London jazz institution, Ray's is for the discerning jazz listener. Impressive arrays of classic jazz and blues are balanced with avant-garde, Afro-Cuban and Latin, and there is a good range of big-band swing, with all the well-known band leaders and singers of their day. The Dorseys, Miles Davis, Jelly Roll Morton and Artie Shaw are some of the big names represented here, and there are sections on male and female jazz vocalists. Records start from £2, and go up to £40 or £50 on the rare LP rack. Black-and-white jazz theme posters go from £14.50. There are also some second-hand books about jazz and new CDs.

Recall Records
28 Sterling Way, Upper Edmonton N18 (0181) 887 0468
The range of records in this shop is good but rather expensive: though some LPs are from £3, most hover around the £6–8 mark. Bowie, the Beatles and Elvis have pretty comprehensive sections, and there's reggae, rock, heavy metal, Seventies and Eighties progressive pop, all the way down to jazz, blues, shows and easy listening. There are some tapes starting at £3, and a shelf of second-hand books on singers and musicians.

Reckless Records
79 Upper Street, Islington N1
(0171) 359 0501
This shop doesn't have a brilliant selection, but its virtue is that it is cheaper than the vast Notting Hill empire's outlets. Categories are industrial, dance, soul, rock/pop, film soundtracks. The Islington branch specializes in mainly rock and pop, with a few classical LPs thrown in. Down in the rarities basement – only open Monday to Saturday – you'll find a good range of soul, contemporary, easy listening, rock and the like from George Michael to deleted soundtracks. The rest of the shop is open seven days a week until 7p.m. Records start at £1.99, CDs at £3.99.

Also at 30 Berwick Street, Soho W1 (0171) 437 4271.

Record Archives
95 Woolwich Road, Greenwich SE10
A brilliant and unexpected little record shop on the outskirts of Greenwich, which sells mostly Fifties, Sixties and Seventies pop albums at low prices (from £2), and a few contemporary shows. It also sells a small selection of videos for around £4, with some fairly recent issues like *Last Exit to Brooklyn* and *Back to the Future.*

Rhythm Records
281 Camden High Street, Camden Town NW1 (0171) 267 0123
Two floors of new and second-hand records, CDs and tapes, featuring reggae, jazz, hardcore, country and western and nostalgia. Concert tickets are also sold from here.

Rock On
3 Kentish Town Road, Camden Town NW1
This small, tatty, quirky little shop next to Camden Town tube station stocks hundreds of records arranged into categories like reggae, Seventies and Eighties British, R&B, soul,

gospel, country, and Eighties and Nineties in a funky atmosphere. LPs are priced from a reasonable £3, 10-inch albums from £2, singles from 50p and 12-inch singles from £1; and small range of tapes starts at £3. Rarer recordings go for more, like a Sanford Clark album for £45, Eddie Cochran at £30, Cowboy Copas for £70, or a Wayne Raney at £100. And there are always plenty of fliers up in the windows telling you what's happening on the music scene. Open seven days a week.

Shakedown
297 Portobello Road, Notting Hill W11 (0171) 964 5135
The cheap and funky little Shakedown shop up beyond the Westway flyover sells a hip mix of punk, Eighties garage, psychedelic, Seventies New Wave, industrial, Gothic, heavy metal, rock and Sixties. The selection is small but good, with prices averaging between £6 and £8 for an LP.

Also at 24 Inverness Street, Camden Town NW1 (0171) 284 2402.

Sidewinder
38 St Martin's Court, Covent Garden WC2 (0171) 240 5060
A tiny shop off St Martin's Lane opposite the Albery Theatre on two floors, specializing in pop music of the last thirty years, with a good selection even though it's somewhat inaccessible. The ground floor has a wall of videos from £4 (including a good selection of pop artists in concert), as well as CDs from £5 (though mostly £7–8), and 12-inch singles for £2. Downstairs are more records arranged into soul, pop, soundtracks, etc., and a reasonably small selection of cassettes. Nothing is in any sort of alphabetical order and it's the type of shop where you could feel slightly intimidated by staff standing close by and watching you. Videos go from £5, three for £12.

Soul Jazz Records
11 Ingestre Place (parallel to Lexington Street), Soho W1 (0171) 494 2004
The second-hand records here average around £10, with names such as George Benson, Blue Note, Miles Davis, Earth, Wind and Fire, Herbie Hancock and Quincy Jones. There's also a rack of £4 cheapies.

Spinning Discs
54 Chiswick High Road, Chiswick W4 (0181) 994 4604
A retro shop fairly close to Turnham Green tube station, stocking a very comprehensive collection of Fifties and Sixties sounds for the hardened cognoscenti. All the big names are here – The Beatles, Eddie Cochran, lots of Elvis, The Fleetwoods, Roy Orbison, Jack Scott and Neil Sedaka; prices start at £5 for LPs, £2.50 for singles, £1 cheapies outside. There are also old pics on the wall, some in mint condition.

Steve's Sounds
20 Newport Court, Covent Garden WC2 (0171) 437 4638
These two small adjacent shops off the Charing Cross Road at the entrance to Chinatown flog second-hand records, tapes, CDs and videos, from contemporary pop and rock to heavy metal, easy listening, classical sounds and soundtracks. It is a haven for those who don't mind standing and flipping through hundreds of albums at lunchtime and maybe not finding what they really want, for the range is so wide and unpredictable that a visit here is worth it. Pop and classical CDs from £4; heavy metal CDs from £3; bargain CDs in boxes outside for 50p; records from £2.50; bargain records from £1 outside.

Tone's Music Store
282 North End Road, Fulham SW6
(0171) 381 3000
In a little purpose-built shop – more of a Portakabin really – on the corner of Croomer Place in front of a once-grand mansion that now serves as a rambling antiques market, this CD specialist sells a range of rock, pop, soul, jazz, soundtrack and classical CDs – along with the odd tape – averaging about £6 each.

Trax
55 Greek Street, Soho W1
(0171) 734 0795
This hyper-trendy place really is for those who really know what they like in up-to-the-minute high-tech dance-beat music. The albums are divided up into categories like Belgian, New Euro, Baleari, German and Dutch techno, Italo classics, current and pop, and Sueño Latino. LPs go for around £3.99 and 12-inch singles from £1.

Unlimited
9 Northwold Road, Stoke Newington N16 (0171) 275 7513
This incredibly noisy shop just off Stoke Newington High Street specializes in reggae, soul, dance, African, gospel, R&B and rarities with a roll-call of names like John Coltrane, Sister Pansly, Chante Moore, Tevin Campbell, Shirley and Lee and Ace Cannon.

Vinyl Experience
3 Buck Street, Camden Town NW1
(0171) 267 5228
Tucked down a side street near Camden Town's covered market in the High Street, this purely second-hand shop stocks mainly punk, new wave, Indie and blues records from £3.99. In the basement via a side entrance in the street, you'll find videos (mainly mainstream Hollywood violence) from £8, and pop/contemporary records.

Also at 15 Hanway Street, Fitzrovia W1
(0171) 636 1281

Vinyl Solution
231 Portobello Road, Notting Hill W11
(0171) 792 9778
This noisy shop has a good collection of noise and industrial, hardcore, Seventies UK and US rock, Elvis, The Beatles, heavy metal and Sixties UK and US pop, averaging about £7 for an album. There are collectibles from the Fifties onwards at various prices, as well as a dance music selection down in the basement.

West End Leisure
17 Praed Street, Paddington W2
(0171) 402 5667
The mainstay of this tatty little shop down from the hospital is videos. You'll find fairly recent titles like *Young Doctors in Love, The Missionary, Wilt* and *Wild at Heart* for £3.99, as well as a range of fitness videos from £4.50. There's also a small selection of contemporary CDs, records and tapes from £2 each.

OTHER OUTLETS

AUCTION ROOMS

The idea of auction houses can put a lot of people off, with their elaborate code of bidding behaviour: it can all seem as gruelling as a public performance in a gentleman's club. But once you crack the system of viewing *and bidding, auctions can be a lot of fun – and a good way of picking up a decent article of furniture, porcelain, painting or the like at a realistic price. Listed below are the days when viewing is possible, days and times of sales and any particular speciality that the auction house deals in.*

AUCTIONS

The mystique of the auction room shouldn't put you off. Firstly, ring up if you want something specific, otherwise show up during the viewing hours and carefully examine the merchandise – it's a strict *caveat emptor* (let the buyer beware) policy, so you buy as seen, defects and all. You can put an offer on anything there and then, and let the auctioneer do your bidding for you – if it comes in less than you've put up front, you will be refunded the difference.

At an auction, always decide how much you want to spend, and stick religiously to it, so that you don't start outbidding yourself and realize you've blown a small fortune. To bid, watch what everyone else is doing first – a discreet wave of the catalogue could be *de rigueur*. If you bid successfully on an article, the auctioneer will usually shout out your name and address and you can settle up once the auction is over. There is usually a buyer's premium of 10 per cent that you must stump up.

Arch Auction Rooms
Unit 4, Deptford Trading Estate,
Blackhorse Road, Deptford SE8
(0181) 694 1656
Sales Alternate Sundays 11a.m.
Viewing Saturday 10a.m.–5p.m.
General household, office and liquidated stocks; antiques, jewellery, collectibles, *objets d'art*.

Bainbridges
St John's Yard, St John's Parade,
Mattock Lane, Ealing W13
(0181) 579 2966
Sales Approximately every six weeks on Thursdays at 10.30a.m.
Viewing Wednesday before sale 1–7p.m.; sale days from 9.30a.m.
General household with a minimum price of £10 for anything. Auctions are held in the Great Barn, Bury Street, Ruislip. Ample parking.

Bloomsbury Book Auctions
3–4 Hardwick Street, Bloomsbury EC1
(0171) 636 1945
Sales Alternate Thursdays 1p.m.
Viewing Tuesday 9.30–5.30p.m. and

Wednesday 9.30a.m.–8p.m.
General books, with some specialist sales.

Frank G. Bowen Ltd
15 Greek Street, Soho W1
(0171) 734 9192
Sales Alternate Thursdays 10.30a.m.–1p.m.
Viewing Monday 9a.m.–4.30p.m., Thursday 9–10.30a.m.
Furniture, toilets, washbasins, jackpot machines, office furniture, desks.

Cambridge Heath Auctioneers and Valuers
Arch 288–289 Cambridge Heath Road, Bethnal Green E2 (0171) 729 4029
Sales Tuesday 7p.m.
Viewing Sunday 10a.m.–4p.m., Monday 10a.m.–5.30p.m., Tuesday 10a.m.–6.30p.m.
General household, some new job lots.

Centaur Auctions
Harbet Road, Edmonton N18
(0181) 803 9796
Sales Alternate Saturdays 10a.m.
Viewing Friday 10a.m.–4p.m., Saturday 9–10a.m.
Office and computer equipment, machinery, trade stocks.

Chiswick Sale Rooms
3 Heathfield Terrace, Chiswick W4
(0181) 742 2240
Sales Tuesday 5p.m. and 7p.m.
Viewing Sunday noon–6p.m., Monday and Tuesday 10a.m.–6p.m.
Carpets, pictures and smalls auction (5p.m.), antiques and furniture (7p.m.).

Criterion Auction Rooms
53 Essex Road, Islington N1
(0171) 359 5707
Sales Monday 6p.m.
Viewing Friday 4–8p.m., Saturday and Sunday 11a.m.–3p.m., Monday 10a.m.–6p.m.
Antique furniture – mainly dining suites, sideboards, some modern pine pieces – decorative items, some china; some good-quality pieces, mostly pre-Thirties and needing some attention.

Forrest and Co
79–85 Cobbold Road, Leyton E11
(0181) 534 2931
Sales Alternate Thursdays 11a.m.
Viewing Wednesday 10a.m.–5p.m., Thursday 10–11a.m.
Household goods, repossessed stock from bankrupt businesses, beds, chairs, fridges, kettles for a few pounds.

Fulham Auction Rooms
460 Fulham High Street, Fulham SW6
(0171) 610 0210
Sales Thursday 6p.m.
Viewing Wednesday 10a.m.–7p.m., Thursday 10a.m.–6p.m.
General household, with an emphasis on antiques.

General Auctions
63 Garratt Lane, Tooting SW18
(0181) 874 2955
Sales Car sales Monday 7.30p.m.
General sales Monday 11a.m.
Viewing Saturday 10a.m.–3p.m.
Good vehicle auctions, general furniture – antique and modern – cycles, bric-à-brac, cameras; very good bankruptcy stock, garage tools, car sales.

Stanley Gibbons Auctions
399 The Strand, Covent Garden WC2
(0171) 836 8444
Sales and Viewing Ring for details.
London's foremost philatelic auctions.

Gray's Auctions
34–36 Jamestown Road, Camden Town NW1 (0171) 284 2026
Sales Tuesday 6p.m.

Viewing Tuesday 10a.m.–6p.m.
General household, jewellery and silver.

R.F. Greasby
211 Longley Road, Tooting SW17
(0181) 672 1100
Sales Alternate Mondays 10a.m.
Viewing Saturday before sale
10a.m.–4p.m.
London Transport and British Airways lost property: umbrellas, baby buggies, suitcases, toys and small electrical articles. Also Inland Revenue and bankrupt hauls.

Harmer's of London
91 New Bond Street, Mayfair W1
(0171) 629 0218
Sales and Viewing Ring for details.
Collectors' postage stamps.

Hatton Garden Auctions
36 Hatton Garden, Holborn EC1
(0171) 242 6452
Sales Jewellery Thursday 11.30a.m.
Silver Thursday 3p.m.
Viewing Monday to Wednesday and Friday 9a.m.–4.30p.m.
Mainly dealers attend, but the public can snap up jewellery, silver items or small furniture items; it's also a pawnbrokers.

Hornsey Auctions Ltd
54–56 High Street, Hornsey N8
(0181) 340 5334
Sales Wednesday 6.30p.m.
Viewing Tuesday 5–8p.m. and Wednesday 9a.m.–6.30p.m.
General antique furniture.

K. & F. Partnership
Lea Valley Trading Estate, Angel Road, Edmonton N18 (0181) 803 9796
Sales Alternate Saturdays 10a.m.
Viewing Friday 10a.m.–4p.m., Saturday 9–10a.m.
General household and vehicles.

Lewisham Auction Rooms
42a Nightingale Grove, Lewisham SE13
(0181) 852 3145
Sales Wednesday and Saturday
11a.m.
Viewing Tuesday and Friday
10a.m.–5p.m.
Mainly executors' and liquidators' sales of general house clearance.

Dowell Lloyd and Co
118 Putney Bridge Road SW15
(0181) 788 7777
Jewellery:
Sales Tuesday 9.30a.m.
Viewing Monday 9a.m.–3.30p.m.
Police, London Taxis and BAA lost property:
Sales Alternate Saturdays 9a.m.
Viewing Friday 9a.m.–7.45p.m.
Metropolitan Police auctions, London Taxis and British Airport Authority: umbrellas, handbags, luggage, cameras, videos, TVs, car radios, bicycles, antique furniture, ceramics, general household items, glassware, beds, carpets, sofas, tables – some of good quality.

Lots Road Chelsea Auction Galleries
71–73 Lots Road, Chelsea SW10
(0171) 351 7771
Sales Monday 4p.m. (contemporary); 6p.m. (antiques).
Viewing Friday 9a.m.–3p.m., Saturday and Sunday 10a.m.–1p.m.
Furniture, pictures, carpets, rugs, glass, ceramics.

MacGregor, Nash and Co
9–17 Lodge Lane, North Finchley N12
(0181) 445 9000
Sales Monday 5p.m.
Viewing Sunday 9a.m.–1p.m., Monday 9a.m.–5p.m.
General antiques.

Thomas Moore Auctioneers
217–219 Greenwich High Road, Greenwich SE10 (0181) 858 7848

Sales Thursday 10a.m.
Viewing Wednesday 2–8p.m., Thursday 9–10a.m.
Georgian, Victorian, Edwardian furniture, porcelain, glass, watercolours and paintings.

Onslow's Auctioneers
Metro Store, Sands Wharf, Townmead Road, SW6 (0171) 371 0505
Sales and Viewing Ring for details.
Specialist transport auctioneers – railway, maritime and aviation memorabilia, as well as travel posters.

James Owen and Co.
136 Granville Road NW2
(0181) 458 5545
Sales and Viewing Ring for details.
Deals in commercial liquidations and holds very irregular auctions; usually around 500 lots. Ring first.

Phoenix Auctions
30 St Aubyn's Road, Crystal Palace SE19 (0181) 768 1672
Sales last Tuesday of month 10a.m.
Viewing Sunday 2–6p.m., Monday 10a.m.–6p.m. before sales
Books.

Regency Auction Rooms
62 St James's Street, Walthamstow E17
(0181) 520 0255
Sales Tuesday and Thursday 6.30p.m.
Viewing Tuesday and Thursday 4.30–6.30p.m.
General antiques and collectibles.

Roseberry's Fine Art
The Old Railway Booking Hall, Station Road, Crystal Palace SE19
(0181) 778 4024
Sales Alernate Wednesdays antiques; alternate Tuesdays general.
Viewing Sunday 2.30–5.30p.m., Monday 10a.m.–7.30p.m.
Quality antiques: furniture, Victoriana, pictures, ceramics and decorative items.

Southgate Auction Rooms
55 High Street, Southgate N14
(0181) 886 7888
Sales Friday 6.30p.m.
Viewing Friday 10a.m.–6p.m.
Behind the Town Hall in a large warehouse are small lots like jewellery, bronzes, paintings, books, china, some larger pieces of furniture.

Spink and Son
5–7 King Street, St James's SW1
(0171) 930 7888
Sales and Viewing Ring for details.
Coins, banknotes and medals from London's oldest coin and medal dealers (established 1666).

CHARITY SHOPS

Set up to raise funds for charities in aid of health, famine victims, housing programmes and other needy causes, charity shops have found their niche in post-Thatcherite Britain, and have gone from necessity to chic. All the charity shops – except Humana with its clothes-only policy – offer a range of bric-à-brac, including records, dishes, books, clothes, and in some cases smaller pieces of furniture. Prices seem to vary according to the whim of the volunteer who prices the donations, and service can be in the doddery-old-granny department. They range from the huge chains of Oxfam or the Imperial Cancer Research Fund to small one-offs like the Relief Fund for Romania, Yjinia Housing Association and the Geranium Charity Shop for the Blind. Oxfam tends to be more expensive and have better quality, but still offers bargains for those who care to seek them out. I swear that Humana is the place in London to buy clothes — especially men's blazers and jackets – and the small one-offs or tiny chains see some top-quality stock at dirt-cheap prices, so dry cleaning the thing you buy might be more expensive than the price you buy it for. The quality varies from Marks and Sparks to well-known French and Italian labels, all at low, low prices. Below are the best charity shops and the addresses of their London outlets.

British Red Cross
The Red Cross movement was founded in Switzerland in 1859 to care for the wounded through a voluntary agency of trained members, and today helps people throughout the world during flood, famine, war and earthquakes, on a totally impartial basis. The main objective of this string of shops is to raise revenue for the Red Cross's refugee support, welfare assistance programmes and care for the elderly and disabled, as well as training and education programmes to equip volunteers who staff first-aid posts at sporting and public events. They haven't mastered the pricing formula like Oxfam or the Cancer Research people, so the stock is very variable and you can pick up some surprising bargains.

49 Station Road, Chingford E4
44a Dalston Lane, Hackney E8

Houndsfield Road, Edmonton N9
6 Muswell Hill, Muswell Hill N10
259 Green Lanes, Palmers Green N13
219 Fore Street, Edmonton N18
600 Holloway Road, Upper Holloway N19
119 Finchley Road, Swiss Cottage NW3
15 Vivian Avenue, Hendon NW4
170 High Road, Willesden NW10

46 Vanbrugh Park, Blackheath SE3
213 Stanstead Road, Forest Hill SE23
54 Ebury Street, Pimlico SW1
71 Old Church Street, Chelsea SW3
106 Clapham Road, South Lambeth SW9
11–12 Bramlands Close, Battersea SW11

332 Kingston Road, Merton SW20

152 Shepherd's Bush Road, Hammersmith W6
35 The Broadway, West Ealing W15

67 Kilburn High Road, Kilburn NW6
Lewisham High Street, Lewisham SE13
102 Peckham Rye, Peckham SE15

TOP-DRAWER CLOTHES

If you're a confirmed charity-shop shopper, concentrate on the posher areas for higher-class cast-offs – try the Imperial Cancer Research Campaign's shops in Highgate, Blackheath or Temple Fortune, Oxfam in Hampstead or the King's Road, or the Red Cross at Swiss Cottage, Wimbledon or Totteridge – designer labels on perfect garments often turn up for a song. And, whatever you do, don't overlook the superlative Humana in Kilburn and Peckham with a huge assortment of varying quality.

Humana
Dealing purely in clothes, the two Humana branches have the atmosphere of a soiled Sunday church hall fête and the smell of damp clothes left on the radiator, but also the widest, most satisfying selection of used garments in London, where you can stumble across a perfect YSL jacket for £8. The musty, tatty stores are crammed with well-sorted racks of men's, women's and kiddies' gear, with separate areas for ties, shoes, handbags and special clearance items for £1. Prices have recently risen: suits now go for £10, trousers from £5, shirts from £2.50, shoes from £5.

Imperial Cancer Research Fund
Europe's largest independent cancer research institute employs 1000 doctors, scientists and technicians to carry out one third of all cancer research in the UK. The 468 voluntary charity shops throughout the country raised £6.5 million towards the £53 million research programme in 1993; the rest of the amount comes from personal legacies. Like Oxfam, they've become wise to market demand, and you won't find the biggest bargains here, with jackets for £10, shirts for £6.50 and suits at £15–18. Enquiries (0171) 269 3615.

55 Old Church Road, Chingford E4
154 High Street North, East Ham E6
96 High Street, Walthamstow E17

31 Upper Street, Islington N1
69 Ballard's Lane, Finchley N3
72 Highgate High Street, Highgate N6
13 The Broadway, Crouch End N8
161 Muswell Hill Broadway, Muswell Hill N10
775 High Road, North Finchley N12
353 Green Lanes, Palmers Green N13
90 Chase Side, Southgate N14
168 Fore Street, Edmonton N18
7 High Road, Wood Green N22
81 Camden High Street, Camden Town NW1
63 Brent Street, Hendon NW4
187 Kilburn High Road, Kilburn NW6
234 West End Lane, West Hampstead NW6
37 The Broadway, Mill Hill NW7
652 Kingsbury Road, Kingsbury NW9
871 Finchley Road, Golders Green NW11
3 Hallswell Parade, Finchley Road, Temple Fortune NW11

6 Montpelier Vale, Blackheath SE3
135 Lewisham High Street, Lewisham SE13
30 Westow Hill, Upper Norwood SE19
101 Sydenham Road, Sydenham SE26
85 St John's Road, Clapham SW4
387 North End Road, Fulham SW6
393 King's Road, Chelsea SW10
168 Balham High Road, Balham SW12
244 Upper Richmond Road West, East Sheen SW14
1390 London Road, Norbury SW16
65 Streatham High Road, Streatham SW16
58 The Broadway, Wimbledon SW19

24 Marylebone High Street, Marylebone W1
278 Chiswick High Road, Chiswick W4
48 The Broadway, West Ealing W5
66 The Mall, Ealing W5
123a King Street, Hammersmith W6

North London Hospice
The North London Hospice in Finchley is solely dependent on voluntary contributions and the charity shops dotted throughout North London contribute. They are small and poky, musty and jumble-sale-like, but where else can you pick up six sherry glasses for £1, books from 50p or clothes from £1? Head office: (0181) 343 8841.

123 High Road, East Finchley N2
35 Highgate High Street, Highgate N6
1271–1273 Whetstone High Road, Whetstone N20
212 High Road, Wood Green N22

Notting Hill Housing Trust
This housing trust was set up in the Sixties to provide affordable rented accommodation to people on low incomes in West London, and now also provides hostel and temporary accommodation. Some of the shops occupy vacant premises and must move at forty-eight hours notice, but the following are permanent fixtures. They tend to be a bit hit-and-miss, as stock varies from week to week and from store to store, and the premises can be a bit tacky and musty, but branches stock the sundry collection of china oddments, records, clothes and toys that people don't want, as well as a range of new Chinese and Indian crafts.

86 Camden High Street, Camden Town NW1
7 High Street, Harlesden NW10

211 Brompton Road, Earls Court SW3
29, 184 and 193 King's Road, Chelsea SW3
411 North End Road, Fulham SW6
4 Northcote Road, Battersea SW11
182 Balham High Road, Balham SW12
288 Upper Richmond Road, Putney SW15
36 High Street, Tooting SW17
19 The Broadway, Wimbledon SW19

63 and 168 Tottenham Court Road, Euston W1
67–68 Piccadilly, Mayfair W1
178 Queensway, Bayswater W2
166 High Street, Acton W3
46 Turnham Green Terrace, Turnham Green W4
31 High Street, Ealing W5
8–10 King Street, Hammersmith W6
57 Kensington Church Street, Kensington W8
175 Kensington High Street, Kensington W8
59 Notting Hill Gate, Notting Hill Gate W11
204 Portobello Road, Notting Hill Gate W11
76 Askew Road, Shepherd's Bush W12
64 Shepherd's Bush Green, Shepherd's Bush W12

Oxfam
With the acceptability of second-hand charity shops on the increase, Oxfam went upmarket, bought its own shops and upped its prices, but still bargains are there to be had. It stocks a varied collection of china, books, clothes, records, as well as new imported Indie crafts; prices are more expensive than other charity shops (jackets £10, shirts £3.99), but the shops are free of that nauseating old-clothes smell. Margaret Thatcher reputedly offloaded her husband Denis' gear at the Sloane Square branch...

21 Old Church Road, Chingford E4
570 Kingsland Road, Kingsland E8
1/7 St James Walk, Clerkenwell EC1

55 Ballard's Lane, Finchley N3
326 Green Lanes, Finsbury Park N4
80 Highgate High Street, Highgate N6
233 Muswell Hill Broadway, Muswell Hill N10
724 High Road, North Finchley N12
40 Chase Side, Southgate N14
46a Stoke Newington Church Street, Stoke Newington N16
836 Green Lanes, Winchmore Hill N21
12a The Broadway, High Road, Wood Green N22
39 Camden High Street, Camden Town NW1
61 Gayton Road, Hampstead NW3
166 Kentish Town Road, Kentish Town NW5
246 West End Lane, Kilburn NW6
50 The Broadway, Mill Hill NW7
120 Golders Green Road, Golders Green NW11
1049 Finchley Road, Temple Fortune NW11

68 Tranquil Vale, Blackheath SE3
85 Eltham High Street, Eltham SE9
15 Warwick Way, Westminster SW1
Development Education Unit, Barnwell Road, Brixton SW2
432 King's Road, Chelsea SW10
58 St John's Hill, Battersea SW11
Astoria Parade, 7 Streatham High Road, Streatham SW16
93 High Street, Wimbledon SW19
110 The Broadway, Wimbledon SW19
365 Kingston Road, Wimbledon Chase SW20

13/13a Marylebone High Street, Marylebone W1
52 Goodge Street, Euston W1
240 Edgware Road, Paddington W2
190 Chiswick High Road, Chiswick W4
99 Broadway, Ealing W5
202b Kensington High Street, Kensington W8
245 Westbourne Grove, Notting Hill W11
23 Drury Lane, Covent Garden WC2

Scope
The former Spastics Society works with individuals and families to provide practical support and help for sufferers of cerebral palsy – amounting to 1 in 400 of the population. As well as dealing with educational, employment, housing, welfare and leisure needs, the society has day-care housing projects, skills development centres and teams of specialist social workers, and funds research into the condition. Its shops sell clothes, records and general bric-à-brac of varying quality. For more information about the shops, ring (0171) 636 5020.

4 Morning Lane, Hackney E9

6 Islington High Street, Islington N1
24 Ballard's Lane, Finchley N3
46 Seven Sisters Road, Holloway N7
304 Green Lanes, Palmers Green N13
236 Stamford Hill, Stoke Newington N16
73 Camden High Street, Camden Town NW1

12 Vivian Avenue, Hendon NW4
139 Kilburn High Road, Kilburn NW6

42 Denmark Hill, Camberwell SE5
2-4 Court Yard, Eltham SE9
50 Eltham High Street, Eltham SE9
7 Lewis Grove, Lewisham SE13
93 Peckham High Street, Peckham SE15
346 North End Road, Fulham SW6

88 High Street, Acton W3

Sue Ryder Charity Shop

A one-time nurse, Baroness Ryder of Warsaw, then Sue Ryder, inaugurated this foundation in the 1950s to ease the suffering of handicapped and homeless children throughout the world. Now the Foundation helps to provide people with homes and hospital care, and runs a series of charity shops, as well as coffee shops and homes, and has spread its net to include support facilities in Ireland, Belgium, Poland and Australia.

101 High Street North, East Ham E6
163 Barking Road, Canning Town E13

17 Liverpool Road, Islington N1
31 The Broadway, Crouch End N8
129 Muswell Hill Broadway, Muswell Hill N10
98–102 Fore Street, Upper Edmonton N18
324 Euston Road, Euston NW1

Surrey Quays Shopping Centre, Lower Road, Rotherhithe SE16
27 Hare Street, Woolwich SE18
16 Church Road, Crystal Palace SE19
52–54 Sloane Square, Chelsea SW1
54 Ebury Street, Pimlico SW1
373 North End Road, Fulham SW6
87 Balham High Road, Balham SW12
108b Streatham High Road, Streatham SW16

38 Margaret Street, Fitzrovia W1
42 Wigmore Street, Fitzrovia W1
22 New Cavendish Street, Marylebone W1
2 Crawford Street, Marylebone W1
72 Westbourne Grove, Paddington W2
229c Chiswick High Road, Chiswick W4
128 Notting Hill Gate, Notting Hill W11
115 Kingsway, Holborn WC2

Trinity Hospice

Trinity Hospice was founded on Clapham Common in 1891 to care for people suffering from advanced illnesses – mainly cancer – and helps patients by controlling their symptoms and with social and psychological support, as in-patients or through day-care or at-home projects. Patients are cared for free of charge, and the charity relies on fundraising for two-thirds of the £2.5 million it costs to run the Hospice. The Hospice's patients come from a wide area of south and west London, and the Hospice, just off Clapham Common, provides a range of services, like education programmes to medical personnel, home care to support families, an on-going social work programme, and a day care service for patients living in the community. The shops are small and not as immaculately organized as Oxfam or Scope, but the bargains here can be impressive. For more information, ring head office on (0171) 622 9481.

77 Streatham Hill, Streatham SW2
9 Old Town, Clapham SW4
174 Clapham High Street, Clapham SW4
389 King's Road, Chelsea SW10
40 Northcote Road, Clapham Junction SW11
107 Balham High Road, Balham SW12
274 Upper Richmond Road, East Sheen SW14

208 Upper Richmond Road, Putney SW15
9 Tooting High Street, Tooting SW17
55 The Broadway, Wimbledon SW19
158 Queensway, Bayswater W2
25 Turnham Green Terrace, Chiswick W4
408 Chiswick High Road, Chiswick W4
23 Notting Hill Gate, Notting Hill W11

JUNK SHOPS

The old-fashioned junk shop is still alive and kicking – although sometimes called a house removal centre, bric-à-brac or second-hand shop – and still brimming over with an unclassifiable array of merchandise, which can be anything from an old record or pair of shoes to a kitchen sink, standard lamp or grandma's chipped crockery. These shops are for hardened second-hand shoppers, the type who love nothing more than to spend Saturday afternoons in combat, fossicking in musty shops in the hope of finding some forgotten heirloom to restore. Purchases in junk shops tend to be the best of second-hand shop bargains – often because owners worry very little about the condition or the quality of their merchandise and they do not specialize in one kind of stock.

Ancient and Modern
380 Brockley Road, Brockley SE4
(0181) 694 9105
Ancient doesn't really feature here – this junk shop deals mainly in really bottom-of-the-market type furniture from the past thirty years – like those Sixties chests of drawers, white plastic-covered wardrobes from the Seventies and sideboards with Formica on the top and glass doors. It is the place for a real bargain, though – make an offer.

The Attic
210a Selhurst Road, South Norwood SE25 (0181) 653 3828
The eyecatching window display trades on the shop's name, and it really does look like the contents of someone's loft space, artfully arranged – an old typewriter, slide projector, an ancient vacuum cleaner, a Singer sewing machine and a few old porcelain vases. Inside, it's more humdrum, with wardrobes from £55, chairs for around £15, pictures at £2 upwards, a stereo perhaps for £75, books for £1, china from £4 and lights from £5. It has a high turnover and low prices.

Bambino
18 Church Road, Crystal Palace SE 19
(0181) 771 5145
This quirky little shop looks like Steptoe and Son's living room, with a ragbag of old junk alongside racks of leather bomber jackets and thigh-length black leather boots. They had a corner wall unit for £50, sunglasses for 50p each, an old carved walnut chair for £30, an old gramophone for £25, a tennis racquet for £10 and an old dressmaker's dummy for £15.

Burke and Hare
113 South Lambeth Road, South Lambeth SW8 (0171) 735 0939
This sinister-sounding house-clearance shop is on the corner of the Old Lambeth Road and has an agreeable, if shabby, collection of junk, such as records from £1, a Sixties dining table for just £20, picture frames from £1, a Fifties dressing table at £55, shelves, old school desks and chairs. Not that good quality, and the furniture needs renovating.

C & G Bargain Shop
15 Lordship Lane, East Dulwich SE22
A small step up from a charity shop,

this wonderful bargain bin of second-hand goodies concentrates on clothes and records, keeping the general bric-à-brac to wade through to a minimum. Men's clothes like jackets at £4, suits for £10, shirts for £2, and women's items like blouses for £2, and skirts at £5 are crammed along the walls on rails. You'll also find quite a few records – 12-inch singles for £1, LPs at £2.50, tapes for £1.99 – as well as videos for around £2.50.

Combined Forces Trust
201 Rushey Green, Catford SE6
(0181) 695 0597
This is really a charity shop, but deserves a mention here because of the large range of sturdy household furniture it stocks. On the relentless Catford one-way system, this shop stocks mainly Fifties and Sixties stuff, especially bigger pieces: sideboards start at £60, wardrobes from £45, kitchen and dining tables from £25, chests of drawers from £20, coffee tables from £15. Books go for as little as 20p for paperbacks, and records from just £1.

Complete House Clearance
89 Rushey Green, Lewisham SE13
(0181) 461 5469
Good for first-time furnishers, this cheap muddle of second-hand furniture, clothes, records and general bric-à-brac is hardly fashionable, but is very good value. Sideboards are around £22, wardrobes £45, small tables £8, bookcases £10, kitchen utensils 50p, books 50p and records £1. You'll find the contents of entire houses here, from lace curtains, pillows and dressing gowns to lamps, tables and cutlery.

Cooks Miscellaneous Stores
159 Praed Street, Paddington W2
(0171) 723 6464
Cooks feature a large range of cameras and the like – they had a Vivitar Automatic for £39, a Petri Racer for £45, an Olympus Trip 35 for £37.50 and a Konica 40mm £110. There are plenty of tapes, with names like the Carpenters, Michael Crawford, Culture Club, Elaine Paige and the Pet Shop Boys for £3, as well as classical CDs at £3, and pop CDs for £4. There are also sundry new items, like scissors, knives, plugs, bottle openers, umbrellas, batteries, cassette decks. All that is second-hand is marked.

Tony and June Davis
23 Battersea Rise, Battersea SW11
(0171) 228 1370
Established forty years ago, this shop has been a permanent Battersea fixture with its rag-bag collection of music boxes, cutlery, pots, pans, china, glass, records, books and odds and sods at bargain basement prices. Downstairs are larger pieces of furniture like a large wooden bookcase for £20, bed heads at £15, a side table for £20 and a Fifties sideboard for just £20.

E.A. Dawson
217 Stoke Newington High Street, Stoke Newington N16 (0171) 254 1056
E.A. Dawson is a bit of a collector, and in his shop is squeezed every concievable type of ornament or incidental, like plaster ballet dancers, china cats, glass decanters, china boxes, an old payphone, flamenco dancer models, clocks, schnapps glasses with brewery slogans and a tin box with a picture of the Queen on the front. It's all cheap and fun, even though it's bewildering shopping here, as there's so much stuff on the shelves. Great news for kitsch fans.

Fentocraw Carboot Shop
35 Tottenham Lane, Hornsey N8
(0181) 347 5235

A charity shop lookalike with similarly low prices and changeable and quirky stock. The unpredictable range of goodies when I was there included a rail of clothes from 50p, a woman's shaver for £8, ice skates £10, an Amstrad turnable for £2, sundry kitchen implements for 50p, a Sony battery-powered casette deck for £10, handbags for £3, a 3-in-1 stereo for £35 and a highchair for £5.

Fiona's Secondhand Shop
97 Burdett Road, Bow E3
(0181) 981 3611
This dirt-cheap second-hand shop has taken over the pavement with its fake log fires, trays, scales, chairs, bowls, curtains and mirrors. You might typically find stacks of records and tapes inside for 50p, oddments of china and glassware from 50p, a pine table for £15, a pushchair for £35, a Creda freestanding oven for £45. Danny's Dog Parlour also operates from here, so be prepared to run into a few animals en route.

J.N. Handley and Sons
19–20 Vincent Road, Woolwich SE18
(0181) 854 7754
Next to the railway line around the corner from Woolwich Arsenal British Rail station is this gem of an antiques shop, set up in 1913 and still dishing up a dizzying collection of antiques, pre-loved bric-à-brac and plain junk. The ground floor has general bric-à-brac, like crockery, cutlery, mirrors, vases, perfume bottles, decanters and oddments from the Sixties that will probably become collectors' items. I picked up a Victorian wooden tea tray for £5, an Edwardian carved plaster mirror for £75 and some hardbound Charles Dickens novels from the Forties for £1 each. Upstairs in one room you might find newer wardrobes for £85 or mattresses for £70; in another huge room heaving with wardrobes, dressing tables, sofas, chests of drawers and dining chairs, all clean and in quite good condition, there was a wing-back chair for £65, a wooden ottoman for £22, small wardrobes from £35 and a Fifties dressing table for £26. The pricing policy here is schizophrenic, so you can pick up some real bargains.

Happyness
37 Essex Road, Islington N1
(0171) 354 9398
A run-down old-fashioned place with varied stock such as an old Polaroid camera, marble salt and pepper shakers, kitchen scales, vases, glasses, assorted mugs, ceramic plant pots, ovens, fridges and frayed bits of carpet. There's a £5 minimum delivery charge locally.

T. Hillyers
301 Sydenham Road, Sydenham SE26
(0181) 778 6361
It's mainly china, glassware, figurines and general household goods you'll find here, not strictly antiques, and some pieces dating from as recently as the Seventies – Cristal d'Arque and things your grandparents own, or that you were brought up with! A cut-glass biscuit barrel was £5, a brown Seventies coffee pot £5, a fluted amber glass fruit bowl £5, a cut-glass cake dish £7 and an Edwardian desk £140.

The Junk Box
151 Trafalgar Road, Greenwich SE10
(0181) 293 5715
This Aladdin's cave of bits and pieces reflects its owner's hoarding instinct, and has shelves filled to the brim with bottles, vases, jugs, candelabras, ornaments, plates, books, records and pictures – some in good condition and of reasonable quality,

others less so. Plates go from £1, wooden boxes from £10, old bottles from £2, records from £2, books from 50p. The highlight of The Junk Box has to be the stacks of ancient dog-eared magazines and newspapers at the back of the shop, including titles like *Film News*, *Tit Bits* and *Musical Express*, all from £2, plus a collection of dramatic old British film stills.

Junk and Disorderly
131 Stoke Newington Church Street, Stoke Newington N16
A real treasure trove or junk centre – whichever way you look at it – this shop has shelves of things that no-one else wants, like ornaments for 50p, kitchen utensils for 10–30p, glasses and cups 30p, albums and tapes for £2, paperback books from 50p, old Tupperware for a song, old library card boxes, jugs, pictures, clothes and clocks.

Kay's
280 King Street, Hammersmith W6 (0181) 748 7288
A dirt-cheap old-fashioned junk shop filled with an amazing collection of shoes, cameras, gravy boats, CDs, rugs, records and tapes, binoculars, vases, clothes, guitars, books, bikes, TVs, kettles, baskets, pens, backgammon sets, games and umbrellas. Phew!

Leslie's House Clearence
105 Roman Road, Bethnal Green E2
This ramshackle little place has piles of clothes, silk-tasselled men's scarves, Homburgs, sequinned gloves, evening gloves, cardboard boxes of saucers, Sixties coffee pots, straw baskets, smaller items of furniture, many well-thumbed Mills & Boon novels, baby clothes ... it's basically a real mess, akin to a nuclear explosion in a clothes factory.

Memories of Mortlake
134 Upper Richmond Road, Mortlake SW14 (0181) 878 4700
This friendly shop full of clutter is a cross between an antiques shop and a charity shop, with plenty of bargains and the odd really nice item. From the walking sticks, plant pots, crockery and picture frames outside, you walk into a space filled with glassware, mirrors, jewellery, racks of clothes, vases, figurines and cutlery, with bedspreads and curtains draped over everything. The owner is a peaceful German lady who keeps her head above it all, and will sell things like a leather briefcase for £10, a wooden frame with mirror for £12, jackets for £10, a cut-glass decanter for £19, an old teapot for £10, a silverplated hair brush for £19, or the odd very good quality antique piece like a stunning Victorian mahogany carved mirror for £295.

Mona Lisa
38 Church Road, Crystal Palace SE19 (0181) 771 7062
An antiques shop crossed with a junk shop. Outside, trestle tables are stacked up with cheap books, jugs, china and ephemera. Inside you'll find a collection of things like a Hitachi wood finish stereo for £30, a chest of drawers for £45, an oak drinks table for £25, mahogany dining chairs for £15 each, or a table and six chairs for £125.

Richard Morgan Antiques
177 Merton Road, Merton SW19
Close to Wimbledon tube station, this small, atmospheric bric-à-brac shop has a startling range of general household goods, like books, tables, trays, old sweet dishes, a huge gilt clock, vases from £2, tableware from 50p, a beautiful crystal chandelier at £120, a Victorian carved chair for £65, books from only 50p or a glass bowl for £5.

Mr Allsorts
191 Northchurch Road, Islington N1
(0171) 704 0982
Vases, glass, pottery, huge elaborate gilt mirrors, the odd dining table and chairs, a chest of drawers, a kitchen dresser, some books and records were some of the items offered in this little house clearance place off the Essex Road.

Len Nash
271 Lillie Road, Fulham SW6
(0171) 381 2450
In this street overloaded with antiques, collectibles and junk shops, this is an old-fashioned removal shop that hasn't succumbed to the temptation of putting its prices through the roof yet like the others. You'll find an array of vases, books, plates, decorative items, chairs, tables, the odd sideboard, candlesticks and so on, all for a reasonable price. It's all upmarket stuff for a house-removal shop and nicely displayed, but a step below what you'd find in an antiques place.

Odds N Sods
323 Brockley Road, Brockley SE4
(0181) 691 8000
This cramped shop stocks anything second-hand, regardless of condition, quality or age. You might typically find a small microwave for £75, a Toyota sewing machine for £85, an Olympus camera for £20, an Amiga typewriter and disc drive for £175, an Amstrad computer printer for £85, old phones, a sofa and clothes.

Oxfam Furniture Shop
23 Streatham High Road, Streatham SW16 (0181) 769 1291
Oxfam's electrical goods and furniture specialist comes as a surprise, and like its mainstream charity shops, the quality here is very mixed. You might find an electric casserole for £24.95, a Morphy Richards hairdrier at £9.95, and a whole host of lamps, lampshades and car radios, as well as tables, chests of drawers, typewriters, stereos and speakers. There was a whole dining suite for £36.95, a bureau for £32.95, car radios from £4.95 and wardrobes from £15.

Also at 570 Kingsland Road, Hackney E8 (0171) 241 4668

Past Caring
76 Essex Road, Islington N1
Mainly second-hand clothes feature here, but there are also some books, along with one-off items like an unusual barley twist lamp for £18, an old Fifties radio for £10, a huge plate for £7, a pottery jug for £5 and necklaces from £3. The clothes are quite cheap, with men's ties at £2, jackets at £8 and dresses at £10.

Pastimes
215 The Broadway, Hanwell W7
A real junk shop on the main road, selling a collection of TV computers, carpets, tapes, pictures, coffee pots, fireplace surrounds, and odd bits and pieces of furniture.

Peter's Furniture Dealers
138 Fortess Road, Kentish Town NW5
This large store has everything from a thermos flask for £1.50 to an Edwardian inlaid cabinet for £250. Prices tend to be a bit high but the selection is interesting and pieces are of good quality, although not necessarily in good condition.

Quasimodos
27 Boston Road, Hanwell W7
(0181) 840 0414
It's the sort of place where you might find a repro dining suite for £100, a black-and-white small portable TV for £12, an armchair for £38, a modern glass/wood wall unit for

£75, a Goldstar microwave for £60, or a Granada colour TV for £60, along with a sundry collection of ornaments, pots, crockery and the like.

Quest Antiques
90 Northfield Road, West Ealing W13
(0181) 840 2349
This is a china and glass specialist stocking a good range of things like vases, plates, bowls and crockery, as well as some nice chandeliers. A solid silver serving set was £135, a brass chandelier £125, a small crystal chandelier £30 or a brass lamp £95.

Scope Antiques
64–66 Willesden Lane, Kilburn NW6
(0171) 328 5833
An antiques shop in Kilburn has got to keep its prices down, and although Scope carries a lot that isn't strictly antique (books, Thirties ornaments and clocks), its bigger pieces are bargains. They had an inlaid tray for £14, a walnut veneer jewellery box for £14, a pair of 18-inch high gilt lampstands for £185, a pair of green velvet, intricately carved Oriental antique chairs for £475, a mirror in wide carved frame for £85, an unusual oak desk with brass inlay at the corners for £175, pictures from £10. There's also an adjacent gallery with a collection of pictures.

The Secondhand Shop
85 Coldharbour Lane, Camberwell SE5
(0171) 737 4379
Near to Loughborough Junction British Rail station and a five-minute walk from Brixton tube station, this junk shop has a large room behind the shopfront piled high with lounge suites, wardrobes, cots, bikes, dressing tables – mostly Fifties and newer. There's a bit of Fifties walnut veneer and plenty of laminated modern stuff, and it's a great place to pick up odds and ends like ironing boards, toasters, pots and pans, washers, driers and fridges. No prices, so make an offer and haggle.

Shirley's House Clearance
373 Roman Road, Bow E3
(0181) 980 5201
Shirley has collected a wide selection of house-clearance goods and crammed them into her little shop. There's an emphasis on glassware of all descriptions: I found a set of six kitsch knobbly blue glass tumblers for £12, a painted porcelain plant pot for £2.95, vases, glass bowls and ornaments for £2.50, a Forties glass jug and six glasses for £18, an old pewter tankard for £4.50, an etched sherry decanter and five glasses for £9, a Minerva bust for £15, a wooden folding chair for £15 and various glass light fittings.

Silvers
94 Mitcham Lane, Streatham SW16
(0181) 769 8603
With a selection of furniture and bits and bobs like vacuums, wardrobes, vases, glasses, teapots, candlesticks, books and velour-covered settee, this unruly shop, established in 1939, can be a great house-filler.

South Bank Removals
355 Wandsworth Road, South Lambeth SW8 (0171) 498 8053
This crowded removals shop has everything you'd expect to find while visiting your old Aunt Betty – crockery, glassware, china, tennis racquets, pictures, books, fluffy toys, clothes, singles and LPs.

Strand Antiques
166 Thames Road, Strand-on-the-Green W4 (0181) 994 1912
A real treasure trove that seems to go on for ever, this antiques shop stocks mainly smaller Victorian pieces, though the odd larger item of

furniture often creeps in. It's set on four levels of a house with general collectibles on the ground floor (pewter candlesticks at £28 a pair), down one level in the scullery are kitchen items like a Victorian iron for £16 and tools like an old plane for £15; out the back in the butler's kitchen are plates from £10, jugs and sugar bowls of every description. Upstairs in the old bedrooms are things such as leather suitcases starting at £15, mirrors of varying sizes and ages from Victorian rococo to an understated oak Thirties model, wooden Victorian boxes, dining chairs and tables for £75, coal scuttles from £25, fireguards from £30, an antique bedspread for £58; in a tiny dressing room are crammed bags from £15, collars, evening shoes with gold sequins from £5, kid gloves from £8. Then finally there are two rooms filled with books: paperbacks from 50p in one, hardbacks from £1 in the other. Picture frames with no glass are abundant up and down the stairs, starting from £10.

David Swan Antiques
358 Brockley Road, Brockley SE4
(0181) 691 1323
This fairly new antiques shop across the road from Crofton Park British Rail station seems to be still finding its feet, as the stock isn't brimming out over the pavement, but they do stock a range of interesting smaller pieces. A cut-glass decanter and six sherry glasses cost around £35, an elaborate carved picture frame – something they have quite a good range of – around £30, a Regency-style chest of drawers £45. Open seven days a week.

225 The Jewellery Exchange Ltd
225 Muswell Hill Broadway, Muswell Hill N10 (0181) 444 9941
This small shop at the intersection with Fortis Green Road stocks a range of second-hand jewellery (necklaces from £4, rings from £3), as well as general knick-knackery: plates from £4.50, paperback books from 50p, mirrors – a good buy with three or four at £25 – pictures from £10, crystal and glassware. You might find something good if you have a keen eye. They're always on the look-out for second-hand jewellery in any condition.

John Tilley Antiques
89 and 93 Catford Hill, Catford SE6
(0181) 690 4650
These two shops a few doors away from each other display an amazing range of lower-end-of-the-market antiques, with lots of china and glassware, as well as silver, vases, old pictures, ornaments and the odd cabinet or standard lamp. Glasses start from 75p, pictures from a few pounds, oil paintings from £45. High-class junk.

Top Drawer Antiques
77 Tottenham Lane, Hornsey N8
(0181) 347 5514
There's some interesting old furniture and collectable items here. When I was there they had a wine table with barley twist legs for £28, a Lloyd loom stool for £28, an inlaid piano stool for £35, an old basket for £10, a silver plated lamp for £14, a pine bookcase for £30, a jug for £2, a teapot for £5, and an oak barley-twist legged table for £120.

MARKETS

London's market tradition dates back two thousand years to the Romans, who set up a trading base close to the Thames. As the city became larger, markets became specialized – Smithfield for cattle and hay, Westcheap for general food, Leadenhall for meat, Cornhill for fish. Some of them still exist, some are remembered only in street names.

The bigger, more popular second-hand markets have become London institutions and tend to be much more expensive than the smaller suburban ones: thus Camden, Portobello and Petticoat Lane markets have a higher mark-up and dealers come along early in the morning and snap up any bargains that there are. And then of course there are the smaller specialist markets which deal in books, stamps or collectibles only, and are very good places to meet fellow enthusiasts or obsessives.

The general rule of thumb for market-going is to arrive early for the real bargains, or hang around at the end and pick up something for a song, and remember that bartering is part of the fun of buying.

Alfie's Antique Market
13–25 Church Street, London NW8
(0171) 723 6066
England's largest covered antiques market has 370 stands on over five floors – some 35,000 square feet. There is a vast array of antiques and collectibles on sale, with particular strengths being decorative antiques, pictures, twentieth-century collectibles and costume jewellery. Dealers are very specialized – whether in posters, advertising paraphernalia, Art Deco metalware, twentieth century furniture or lighting. It's not a cheap place, but most of the merchandise is top quality, quite unusual and worth the price. There is also a licensed restaurant with an outdoor terrace on the roof.

Tuesday–Saturday 10a.m.–6p.m.

Bell Street Market
Bell Street, off Edgware Road, Lisson Grove NW1
This market, in a little backwater off the Edgware Road just over the Marylebone flyover, has been offering antique book enthusiasts a weekend outlet for years. The book part of the market has faded considerably, as many of the bookshops along here have packed up their volumes and left, but a few still eke out a living. A few dozen stalls line the road from the main Edgware Road to Lisson Street. It's a low-key market, and not the high quality that you would expect to find in Chelsea, but it's relaxed, friendly and unknown. Along with books, other stalls feature cheap antiques like furniture and clothes, as well as some dusty old bric-à-brac.

Saturday 7a.m.–2p.m.

Bermondsey Market (New Caledonian Market)
Bermondsey Square, Long Lane, Bermondsey SE1
Opened in the mid-nineteenth century, this was originally a cattle market in Islington, and soon became a popular junk and antiques market late in the Victorian era, attracting huge crowds. After the Second World

War, it transferred to Bermondsey and took on a very different flavour. Today, this is London's premier and most serious antiques market, so dealers roll up from all over the south-east early in the morning, and all the really serious trading happening by torchlight. They finish their trading here by 8a.m. or 9a.m., when the tourists from over the river start to arrive and swell the numbers, until the market gets really busy, so it pays to get here as early as possible. Most of the antiques appear a few weeks afterwards in Islington showrooms with a 300 percent mark-up.

The quality here is high, and the merchandise takes in late Georgian, Victorian and Edwardian pieces, with all kinds of furniture, silver, china, glassware, books, ceramics and collectable items on offer.

Friday 7a.m.–2p.m.

Brick Lane Market

Brick Lane, Shoreditch E1

This throwback to London's pre-gentfried street markets has no frills and often involves wading through mounds of rubbish; the upside is it's real, and the prices reflect this down-to-earth quality. It's really big on atmosphere and always has traders shouting each other down.

The main road is brilliant for fresh fruit and veg, dirt-cheap household goods from washing-up liquid to batteries, with a cosmopolitan air thanks to the many Bangladeshi immigrants. It is also home to the rag trade, with many cheap clothes stalls.

For second-hand odds and bobs, Cheshire Street off to the right is the place for furniture, electrical goods, shoes, crockery, pushbikes, jewellery, clothes, books, camera equipment and small items of furniture. Underneath the railway arches are some musty old junk shops, with glassware and china for next to nothing, furniture like a bureau for £15, or a bookcase for £30, ragbags of fake jewellery from 50p, clothes like shirts for £2, coats for £10 and jackets for £5. I saw a Singer sewing machine on a wooden table for £35, hats for £3, nearly-new folding wooden chairs for £8 and sidetables for £6.

Sunday 8a.m.–1p.m.

Camden Passage Market

Camden Passage, off Upper Street, Islington N1

Camden Passage market was set up only in 1960 while Islington was still a reasonably down-at-heel area, and the next two decades saw the business boom. Today, the pedestrianized passage is lined with pricy antique shops and snooty restaurants, but the market still has some affordable collectable items.

Its market is rather half-hearted, with clusters of activity around Pierrepont Row and where the passage crosses Charlton Place. Antique shop owners and dealers trade cheaper antiques and clothes, records, books, jewellery, Victorian boxes from £20, cigarette cards, old phones at £30, silver cutlery, rugs and shoes. On Thursdays, the two squares have slightly overpriced £2–3 paperbacks, not in brilliant condition. But it is an atmospheric spot, paved and lined with Georgian buildings, and there are plenty of cafés round about to make a morning's browsing memorable. The shops along Camden Passage themselves are a joy to see – very pricy, aimed at straying American and Japanese spendthrift tourists and brimming over with outrageous antique finery.

Antiques *Wednesday 10a.m.–2p.m. and Saturday 10a.m.–5p.m.*

Books *Thursdays 10a.m.–5p.m.*

Camden Town Market
Stables Market, Chalk Farm Road; Electric Ballroom, 184 Camden High Street; Covered Market, Commercial Place, Camden High Street; Canal Market, Camden High Street, Camden Town NW1
Camden's weekend market has become an institution among the leftie trendies who pack the high street with their top-to-toe black ensembles and carefully cultivated downtrodden look. But it's not the bargain hunter's paradise it used to be when it first opened in 1973, and dealers have moved in and upped prices, often forgetting that a load of old tat is still a load of old tat no matter how high the prices. It is, however, a young, buzzy place to spend an afternoon, if you don't mind crowds and the self-consciously trendy.

Best and cheapest of it is the rambling **Stables Market** in Chalk Farm Road, which snakes around old Victorian stables (which used to house canal horses) and opens out on to cobble-stoned squares between the railway line, the main road and the canal. Secondhand clothes stalls line the path running alongside the outside wall, with lots of tweed jackets, leather, suede and fur, 501s and shoes. Much of it is tatty and overpriced, but you can still dig out a bargain if you're not intimidated by stallholders standing over you. The indoor market in the main stable building is a vast barn with dozens of trestle tables with traders displaying an array of glassware, china, lighting, books, pictures and general collectibles, and two stunning rooms devoted to Fifites decor.

Camden Lock Market is based around the railway arches. Stalls are crammed in everywhere between the rail lines, and the arches are used as showrooms for antique rug traders, general furniture, clothes and suitcases. Names like Archive Clothing, Collectors' Arch and Eastern-Western Antiques have a permanent place there, and although not dirt cheap, carry some unusual stock. Further down by the canal are places to sit and eat, and dozens of new craft stalls selling everything from jewellery to posters. The heavily renovated New Market Hall contains even more shops and stalls with new arty and crafty goods. Opposite, all the way along Chalk Farm Road has been taken over by second-hand furniture and clothes shops. There are around six food stalls selling Mexican food, hot dogs and Chinese takeaways.

The **Electric Ballroom** is an indoor basement market on the High Street which offers second-hand clothes, from battered jeans to evening wear. It operates as a club on Friday and Saturday nights, but on Sundays sells an array of jewellery, second-hand and new designer clothes, records and the like. There's also a small café.

The **Covered Market** on the High Street and Buck Street crossing is more souk-like, with dozens of mostly clothes stallholders under canvas. It can get very crowded and narrow walkways crammed with people trying on clothes can get a bit squalid, but atmosphere is all. You'll find 501s from £10, tweed jackets from £15, denim jackets for £25, some CDs and records.

On the east side of the High Street, just over the bridge, is the **Canal Market**, where, amid the Indian jewellery and crafty stuff, are some excellent second-hand stalls. The men's clothes and shoes stall at the end of the covered walkway is a real find, selling shoes for £20 and jackets for £15. In the square is a stall specializing in old sewing machines, typewriters and radios, just by the entrance to the indoor section of the market. Inside are rows selling much dross – wade through the CDs, magazines, photos, postcards and general bric-à-brac before you hit the good clothes section with excellent jackets, waistcoats and dresses from the Fifties onwards.

Stables Market *Saturday and Sunday 10a.m.–6p.m.;*

Electric Ballroom *Sunday 10a.m.–5p.m.;*

Covered Market *Thursday–Sunday 9a.m.–5.30p.m., Thursday and Friday second-hand clothes and bric-à-brac, Saturday and Sunday more style conscious vintage clothes and ethnic/contemporary jewellery;*

Canal Market *Thursday–Sunday 10a.m.–5p.m.*

Chelsea Antiques Market
245–253 King's Road, Chelsea SW3
This indoor market has a range of second-hand clothes, old books, photographs, prints, bric-à-brac, silver, wine glasses, decanters, ornaments, posters, china plates and jewellery in a rabbit warren of a place that gets quite chilly in winter, but does have a friendly atmostphere.

Monday to Saturday 10a.m.–6p.m.

Covent Garden Market
The Piazza, Covent Garden WC2
The covered market at Covent Garden is no longer the pulp of day-old lettuce leaves and East End fruiterers catcalling to passers-by that it was. Since the fruit and veg market that had been there for years moved to South Lambeth in 1972, the market in the piazza has been transformed into a sparkling showpiece of what tourists like to think London is like.

It's serious business on Mondays, with dealers who really know their stuff manning the beautifully presented stalls – everything is artistically arranged on swathes of velvet to be as pleasing to the eye as possible. The market caters largely for the lost-looking tourists milling through Covent Garden, but if you don't mind shelling out above the odds, the experience is a pleasant one: there's always an impromptu string quartet or oom-pah-pah band striking up as you weave in and out of the aisles of goodies, and the merchandise is perfect for birthday presents. There's a wonderful teddy bear stall with dozens of furry comforters of all ages; a stall specializing in old Russian money; silverware, tea caddies, china, pottery, crystal, decanters; mounted prints of Olde England scenes from £10, watches and jewellery; a stall selling silver only – gravy boats, sugar bowls, spoons of various sizes, serviette rings, hip flasks, picture frames; a stall of printer's blocks for £3–4; legal documents from George IV's and Charles II's time; antiquarian books like a late eighteenth-century Bible, or a 1907 set of Shakespeare on handmade paper. The market spreads to the Jubilee Hall to the south, where there is a miscellany of bric-à-brac.

Monday 9a.m.–5p.m.

Exmouth Market
Exmouth Market, off Farringdon Street, Clerkenwell EC1
Parallel to Rosebery Avenue coming out on Farringdon Street, this market is one of London's least known. It's cheap, even though the Clerkenwell area is up and coming, and even though it's lost its edge as people have moved out and the area becomes more office orientated, there is a real, earthy feel to the place; it's also very small and understated. There are a few second-hand

furniture shops along it; also a dozen or so racks of pre-worn clothes like tweed jackets, T-shirts, jeans, suede and cotton jackets, and a stall of military gear with khaki jackets, trousers, camouflage shirts; stalls with hardback books on subjects like history, art, geography, as well as a bargain stall with all books for 50p, or 3 for £1. The bric-à-brac runs to things like records at £1, small tables, pictures, ornaments and old crockery for next to nothing.

Monday–Saturday 9.30a.m.–4.30p.m.

Farringdon Road Market
Farringdon Road, near Cowcross Street, Clerkenwell EC1
Since it was set up in the mid-nineteenth century, Farringdon Road market has dealt almost exclusively in books and manuscripts. It's an odd location – in the gutter of one of London's widest, busiest thoroughfares from Blackfriars to King's Cross, just south of Clerkenwell Road. Now there is only a handful of stalls that still trade, but the tradition is still there. You'll find all nature of old books here – many hardbound, with interesting bindings.

Monday–Friday 11.30a.m.–2p.m., Saturday 9.30a.m.–1p.m.

Grays Antique Market
58 Davies Street, Mayfair W1
Grays is like an antiques nightmare: a plush complex of over 200 neat-as-a-pin stalls displaying their antique finery, with a bubbling stream running through the middle of it all. It's aimed at wealthy tourists and is a very specialized place: where else would you venture to puchase a medieval thimble, some antique Scottish agate, antique textiles, fine English pottery, or Art Deco jewellery? The displays are marvellous and some of the smaller articles are within wallet's reach.

Monday–Friday 10a.m.–6p.m.

Greenwich Market
Open-air market Greenwich High Road; Village Market, Greenwich High Road; Covered market, Market Square, Nelson Road, Greenwich SE10
Greenwich is a strange area. The concentration of shops around what is essentially an aggressive one-way system makes it rather unfriendly for shoppers, as it strives to be a south London Camden Town. But it is a charming place, and the markets here are a lot friendlier, less commercialized and much cheaper. The craft market takes up the covered cobbled Market Square with its wooden watch and hand-painted waistcoat brigade, and the other markets lie along the High Street at different points.

The **main open-air market** lies on the High Road in a semi-circular piazza sandwiched between the modern Greenwich Cinema and a long-stay car park, and here traders set up their clothes, bric-à-brac and furniture stalls. You'll find plenty of records, dinky ornaments, medals, china jugs and sugar bowls, hand mirrors, jewellery, postcards, and bits and bobs your granny used to own but you never quite figured out what she did with them. There are larger pieces of furniture at the back of the square, pouring over into the car park, and you can find some decent dining tables, wardrobes or mirrors if you look carefully. Good quality tweed jackets, coats, dresses and shirts have a few stalls, and there are a few rug stalls with stock of dubious quality.

Next door is the **Village Market**, formerly the South London Antique and Book Centre, in what looks like an old fire station at the junction of the High Road and Nevada Street. It now houses a number of stalls hemmed in together on the ground floor, selling an arty-crafty collection of new stencils, jewellery, pictures made out of bits of pastel-shaded material and bows, and the like. It's all a bit claustrophobic.

Upstairs is a collection of second-hand books, posters, records and videos, along with an eating place called The Crêperie, making the upstairs floor rather smoky.

Around the warehouse is a rambling open-air market – to the left of the building and around the back being very cheap new clothes, becoming a second-hand market around the right-hand side and at the rear. Here you'll find stalls selling Levis from £16, old phones, mirrors, furniture and general tat on dozens of stalls in and out of the small outbuildings at the back.

It may all seem a wee bit church-fête-like compared with Camden Town, but you can make use of Greenwich's olde-worlde tea shops and pubs when you've finished.

Open-air market *Saturday and Sunday 9a.m.–6p.m.*

Village Market *Saturday and Sunday 9a.m.–5p.m.*

Covered market *Saturday and Sunday 9a.m.–6p.m.*

Hackney Wick Market

Greyhound Stadium, Waterden Road, Hackney Wick E15

In a pretty barren road, this weekly car-boot sale draws plenty of crowds and features as many people with full bootloads who want to sell their treasure – no licence is needed, just a £10 deposit on the car space. You'll find people getting ride of their old stereo equipment, furniture, toys, books, clothes, fridges, with cookers from £25 and vacuum cleaners from £10. Remember that there are no guarantees, and that you won't be able to come back next week and find your stallholder again. There are plenty of new household products, with second-hand tapes, clothes from £1.99, kitchenware, toys, computer games and food in evidence, a few furniture stalls, a small selection of whites, records from £1, videos from £1.50 and computer games from around the same price.

Sunday 9a.m.–2p.m.

Kensington Market

49–53 Kensington High Street, Kensington W8

This trendy indoor market on two floors has mainly new clothes, but also some second-hand stuff – there's American Seventies clothes for men and women, classic Fifites wear, some second-hand records, as well as a marvellous bric-à-brac stall.

Monday–Saturday 10a.m.–6p.m.

Kingsland Road Market

Kingsland Road, Dalston E8

Started last century as a market for spare parts, this market is still good for the odd mechanical gadget. But it has diversified and it offers books and bric-à-brac at low prices among the washing-up liquid, fruit and veg – you might find amps, bikes for £25 or a cassette recorder at £25.

Saturday 9a.m.–5p.m.

London Bridge Market

London Bridge British Rail station concourse, Southwark SE1

Strictly for those with a fetish for small collectibles, the forecourt at London Bridge British Rail station turns itself over to a network of trestle tables laden with medals, stamps, banknotes, prints, jewellery, ration books, cloth badges, photos of movie stars, records, tapes and CDs, pub jugs, old copies of *Picture Post*, matchbook covers, and general bric-à-brac like vases, ashtrays and jewellery.

Monday–Saturday 10a.m.–4.30p.m.

Picketts Lock Market

Leisure Centre, Picketts Lock Lane, off Meridian Way, Edmonton N9

A large indoor antiques market with very mixed goods ranging from some genuinely good-quality Victorian furniture to bits and pieces that someone's cleared out of their loftspace. Lots of plates, repro furniture, picture frames, odd milk jugs, a few jewellery stands, cake stands, and the like. Much of it is questionable antique-wise, but I bought a Victorian mahogany writing box in reasonable condition which needed a bit of work for £25.

First Sunday of the month 11a.m.–5p.m.; £1 admission.

Portobello Road Market

Portobello Road, Notting Hill W11

There's been a market here since the 1880s, although antiques have only been the primary feature since the 1950s. The world's best antiques market today features over 2000 stall holders on Saturdays and over a mile of trading space from Chepstow Villas in the south to Golborne Road in the north.

From Chepstow Villas up as far as Lonsdale Road, the market has been turned over to the antiques trade on Saturdays, when furniture, jewellery, tableware and sundry silver items are for sale; it's all quite pricy, even though the quality is fairly good, but it's very much geared towards the tourist trade, and the dealers running the stalls certainly won't let a valuable slip through their fingers at less than the market price.

From Lonsdale Road to Lancaster Road, fruit and veg (Monday– Saturday) are the go, with a good Caribbean presence promising some exotic produce, and from Lancaster Road to Westway are general new household items, along with a lot of new clothes (Friday and Saturday), and some dirt-cheap second-hand gear.

North of Westway up as far as Oxford Gardens is where you find the record stalls, along with a bit of general bric-à-brac; north of Tavistock Road, the market becomes really tatty, with bric-à-brac during the week, including clothes, costume jewellery, toys, pictures, books, glass, cigarette cases, gramophones, gas masks, second-hand clothes and porcelain. Right at the top end and along Golborne Road, there's some real tat – things you look at and wonder who on earth would part with cash for them.

Less crowded on a Friday, although there are more stalls on Saturday. The best bargains are gone by 10a.m.

General clothes and bric-à-brac
Friday 8a.m.–3p.m., Saturday 8a.m.–5p.m.

Antiques *Saturday 8a.m.–5p.m.*

Riverside Walk Market

Outside the National Film Theatre Café, under Waterloo Bridge, Southwark SE1

This low-key book market hiding under Waterloo Bridge has been attracting browsers since it was opened in the 1980s, and makes a perfect foil for the ugly South Bank complex, whose attendees mill around during intervals. There are plenty of old prints and books.

Saturday and Sunday 9.30a.m.–5p.m.

INDEXES

INDEX OF SHOPS – ALPHABETICAL

INDEX OF SHOPS – AREA

NORTH LONDON

NORTHWEST LONDON

SOUTHEAST LONDON

SOUTHWEST LONDON

WEST LONDON

EC

EAST LONDON

INDEX OF SHOPS – GOODS